BOOK PUBLISHING
A Working Guide

BOOK PUBLISHING

A Working Guide
for
Authors, Editors
and Small Publishers

by
Donald R. Armstrong

D. Armstrong
Book Printers & Publishers
2000M Governors Circle • Houston, TX 77092
Book Printers & Publishers Since 1960
For information call: 1-(800)-83-BOOKS

713/ 688-1441

5720

Table of Contents

Introduction

"The world is full of people with something to say and with no means to say it, and other people who speak beautifully but have nothing to say . . ."

Ken McCormick
Bowker Lectures on Book Publishing

People with something to say! Those very special individuals who are willing to share their skills, knowledge, experiences, and truths with the rest of us. They come from every walk of life; from every social, economic, and intellectual environment. Many are leaders within their selected areas of expertise, but few are, or have reason to be, 'professional writers of books.'

Herein lies the problem—and the reason this book was written.

Having something worthwhile to say—that satisfies the needs and wants of intended readers—is crucial to the authorship of books. Yet, year after year thousands of important books fail to reach the sales potential they deserve, and tens of thousands of potentially worthwhile manuscripts are rejected.

I have worked, as a book printer and publisher, with hundreds of authors and produced thousands of titles over the past 25 years. I am convinced that at least half of all rejected manuscripts, and fully two-thirds of those published with only minimal success, are caused by *inadequate knowledge and awareness of the book industry itself.*

The book industry is controlled by the laws of economics, and they are severe and unyielding. It is intricately organized, highly specialized, and steeped in rules, procedures, and traditions. There are 'right' ways of doing things—many of which may seem absurd to outsiders (and some are)—but they can only be ignored at great risk. Whether by ignorance or defiance, the consequences are usually the same; the manuscript is never published or, if published, is never exposed to more than a small segment of its potential readers.

It is my hope—and belief—that this book will help you change the odds, presently weighted so heavily against you, in your favor. There are few greater tragedies than for a truly worthwhile book to die, unpublished and unread, in its creator's drawer.

* * *

Here are some of the areas we will explore:

The Industry. The book industry is changing, rapidly. We will take a look at many of these changes and consider their effect on you and on the possibilities for your book. We will look at the industry's organization, requirements, problems, needs, and traditions.

It is a paradoxical industry. To many it creates an image of elitism and aloofness. Yet, there is probably no other industry so open, so helpful, to aspiring entrants; so willing to share its experiences.

Alternatives. There are more than 7,000 publishers in this country, but they operate in very different ways. Some produce books developed exclusively by their own staffs; others work only with literary agents and will never consider an unsolicited manuscript. Almost all specialize, in one way or another, and sending the wrong manuscript to the wrong publisher is a tragic waste of time, money, and energy. So you must know how to pick the publisher that is best for you.

There are *subsidy publishers*, many of whom also act as trade publishers. In spite of the notoriety that subsidy publishers (also known as 'vanity presses') have received, they often serve special needs and may be just right for some authors.

Self-publishing is currently the fastest growing segment of the book industry. With trade publisher rejections running 100:1, increasing numbers of authors are turning to this important alternative—and many are finding profit, satisfaction, and recognition from their choice.

The *small press movement* is providing a creative outlet for thousands of writers whose talents, abilities, and interests also embrace arts, crafts, mechanics, and marketing. These very special people are determined to say their own thing in their own way, and to control the manner in which their message is produced and presented to their selected audiences.

Manuscript Preparation. Whatever alternative may be chosen by an author, he must understand how manuscripts are prepared, processed, edited, and used. The manuscript is the heart and soul of the book, and it must be accurately interpreted by all of those skilled craftsmen who will attempt to convert it into a fine book. Poorly prepared manuscripts are probably the single greatest cause of rejections and a major contributor to errors, redos, and cost overruns.

Book Design and Production. A basic knowledge of the way books are produced is valuable to every author—and essential to the self-publisher. This includes typography, design, illustrations, pagination, camerawork, presswork, and binding. We will also explore the many new and fascinating technologies that are dramatically changing the ways that books are produced: laser printers, optical scanners, graphic scanners, teletypesetting, computer interfacing, word processors, desktop publishing, and more. They should all be generally understood and considered as to their implications on prices, spcifications, and delivery requirements.

Marketing. However well a book may be written and produced, however important the subject covered, if it is not marketed energetically and to the right readers, it will fail to reach its full potential. Marketing is more than persuasion. Especially with books, the mechanics of marketing must also be understood, and the wide range of free publicity that is available must be utilized. But you must know where it is, how to reach it, and how best to make it serve you.

* * *

You will find answers and information about all of these areas, and more, in the pages that follow. They will combine to help you reach a single goal: placing the finest book possible in the hands of the maximum number of readers.

Don Armstrong

Chapter 1

Trade Publishing

Trade publishers are the foundation of the book industry. They edit, produce, and market the vast majority of all books published. A trade publisher speculates. He invests his money, time, resources, and reputation in the books he agrees to publish, and he assumes the full responsibility for his gamble. If the books he offers sell well, he will recover his costs and make a profit. Sometimes he finds himself with a runaway best seller, and the profits can be enormous. But at least half the time he guesses wrong, and loses money. Whatever the result, he guesses—supported by as much judgment, intuition, experience, and scientific data as he can put together.

Authors—especially established, professional authors, with a reputation and a following—are the life blood of trade publishing. There would be no book industry without them.

Authors may work with only one publisher, or they may work with several. They may develop books based on their own ideas, or they may work on assignment on ideas suggested by the needs of their publisher. Some established authors contract with publishers on the basis of nothing more than an outline and a synopsis of the book they plan to write;

others receive contracts only after their books have been completed and accepted. Many authors work on a royalty basis; others for a fee or by outright purchase of their manuscript.

Most trade publishers subcontract most of the actual production of the books they publish to others. Typesetting, printing, and binding are usually handled by book production specialists who provide such services to the industry. However, many publishers will produce at least their own typesetting in-house; others may own or control their own printing facilities which are often operated as subsidiaries or independent entities.

Marketing

Marketing facilities and methods vary significantly between trade publishers. The very large, old, and well-established firms usually maintain experienced and skilled advertising departments. They often have their own sales force which maintains regular, personal contact with major booksellers on a national basis. They also maintain close relations with book reviewers and editors of major newspapers, magazines, and other publications. They know, and are known by, most national and big-city radio and television talk-show hosts. Many advertise in book-oriented publications, such as *Publisher's Weekly*, *New York Times Book Review*, and others. For such publishers the marketing activity is handled like a giant, creative production line: new books are fed in one end, to come out, in due course, at the other, fully garmented and ready for acceptance by the buying public.

But this is not always the case. Economics and potential risks play a major role in the marketing commitment. Even among the largest publishers, advertising and promotion are carefully budgeted in relation to each book's promise for success. The largest budgets and the most elaborate promotions are allotted to those new titles with the greatest sales potential, usually based on the track record of the author. Books by lesser known authors may be considered as fillers, with promotional budgets limited to 10 percent (or less) of the list value of the first printing.

Datus C. Smith, Jr. offers the following observations in *A Guide to Book Publishing*:

"Promotion of some kind is an obligation of every publisher for every single book he brings out. If he is not going to take vigorous steps to tell the world about the book, and to help the proper readers for that kind of book understand why they should buy it, the author might just as well have published the book himself . . . [However] the general rule of book promotion is to support [only] the books showing promise . . . he (the publisher) may *regretfully have to decide to spend no more promotional money on books that failed to move.*"

Donald MacCampbell, a successful New York literary agent for thirty-five years, comments in *The Writing Business*:

"*Publishers' publicity departments are notoriously ineffective* . . . because [they have] too many books to promote at any one time, so that not enough attention can be devoted to any one unless it be by a *big-name author* whose work is likely to become a best seller. . . . A book that dies before its date of publication is not likely to be revived thereafter. . . . lesser known writers are simply carried along for the ride while *the bulk of the company's energy is devoted to securing enormous sums for the subsidiary rights to books by the 'big names.'* . . . Booksellers do not want to load up on fillers. They tend to siphon off the top three or four titles of a publisher's list and *ignore unknown names—especially first-time novelists.*"

Geographic Location

The vast majority of all U.S. trade publishers are located in the New England area, but increasing numbers are in California. Other states with a significant number of book publishers are: Illinois, Florida, Texas, Wisconsin, Ohio, and Michigan. By any measure, New York and the states surrounding it continue to constitute the book capital of the United States.

What does this mean to the new author living in Oklahoma or Louisiana?

The realities of any industry—whether it is motion pictures, television, electronics, or book publishing—suggest that, all things equal, those industry members located 'where the action is' usually receive priority consideration. This tendency is underlined by Edward Weeks, a leading editor of the industry, relating his earlier experiences as an editor of *Atlantic*:

> ". . . it was my hope to discover for the magazine as much new talent as possible. I did this by *working on those friends of mine who were beginning to write; they in turn referred me to their friends*, and I followed every likely lead that offered."

Another well-known editor, Ken McCormick, has made the following observation:

> "There are fewer unsolicited manuscripts accepted by publishers today because it is almost impossible for any talented individual to write much without being observed. He is approached by the publisher, an agent, or a friend who *knows* a publisher or agent."

It is also significant that fifteen of the sixteen U.S. colleges and universities listed by *Barron's Profiles of American Colleges* as being 'most competitive' are located within a 300 mile radius of New York City. The long-term implications of this fact alone—with respect to friendships, contacts, and loyalties—are enormous and pervasive.

Do these facts imply an impenetrable clique that cannot be joined from afar? No. New and successful writers surface every year from virtually every geographic region and from every kind of environment.

But it is important to recognize the realities as they are. The geographically isolated writer will probably find it more difficult to gain initial acceptance and recognition. The value of friendships and a wide web of influential contacts and acquaintances cannot be discounted. The intellectual vigor and enthusiasm radiating from such individuals can be tremendously stimulating and educational. The tidbits of information and the opportunities uncovered by such daily exposures can be extremely valuable. Example:

> "Late in 1965 a Putnam editor stopped in at Magazine Management's offices, overheard Puzo (Mario Puzo, author of *The Godfather*) telling Mafia yarns and offered a $5,000 advance for a book about the Italian underworld. The rest is publishing history."
>
> (*Time*, August 28, 1978)

Does it follow that every aspiring writer should beat a trail to New York? Quoting Ken McCormick again:

> "Writers who should be encouraged to stay at home and keep up their writing are encouraged to come to New York City, where they lose the one thing they had to offer: *a feeling of their own grass roots.*"

The Small Publisher

Fortunately—for new writers—the book publishing industry is changing and expanding rapidly. New publishers are springing up all over the country, and in California a literal publishing revolution has long been underway. Most of the newer publishers are small and the majority publish less than 25 titles annually. But they are growing at disproportionately rapid rates. Most of these new publishers are fired with enthusiasm for the possible and bring to the industry a new sense of creative imagination and innovation.

Smaller trade publishers are faced with many problems. They usually do not have large financial resources to gamble, even if they choose to do so. Most do not have the same connections, especially on a national basis, with the major influencers and personalities that can stimulate a new book's rapid acceptance. Few have their own direct sales force, and those that do rely on direct sales efforts are often restricted to free-lance commissioned sales agents and jobbers. Many depend almost exclusively on mail advertising to sell their books to clearly identifiable markets.

A small publisher is obviously limited as to the number of

new titles and authors he can accept in a given year, which may lower an unpublished author's chances for acceptance. On the other hand, a large publisher, publishing many titles by many well-known authors in a wide range of subject categories may not be able to give a new author the attention his book deserves. The question may be whether one chooses to be a big fish in a small pond or a filler between large numbers of established, prominent authors. There are obvious advantages and disadvantages to each.

Most newer and smaller publishers are well aware of their weaknesses and are turning them into strengths. Their very smallness gives them the capability for deciding fast and moving fast—which in turn helps them respond more quickly to changing needs and opportunities. Not being obligated to, or dominated by, the established literary giants, they can be more creatively receptive to that ever-growing crop of new talent developing throughout the land. Being small, they can avoid the endless chain of judgmental delegation inevitable with bigness. The originating principals can be personally and intimately involved in every author contact, every manuscript decision, and every marketing opportunity.

Specialization

Most publishers tend to specialize in certain kinds of books. This is especially true of smaller publishers. They can—and most do—cut out definable segments of the market that fit their personal philosophies, interests, experiences, and enthusiasms, and focus their resources and energies toward that market. By doing so they can develop a degree of expertise and in-depth coverage of their selected areas that would be impossible otherwise.

Publishers specialize in one or more of the following general areas: fiction, nonfiction, juveniles, textbooks, hobbies and crafts, reference, technical, scientific, medical, education, religion, business, etc. In addition, however, many publishers pursue specific specializations within such areas. For example, in the area of radical feminist novels. Some publishers also announce 'special needs' from time to time—subject areas for which they believe a market exists and on which they are interested in receiving queries or manuscripts.

Most publishers print general catalogs which list and describe the books currently in their backlist. Supplemental catalogs are also available several times each year which include new and forthcoming titles. These catalogs offer an excellent way to get a 'feel' for each publisher's policies and interests. You may also uncover clues to any 'holes' that may exist in a publisher's backlist.

Most catalogs are free; a few publishers charge from $.25 to $1.00. Always include a stamped, self-addressed envelope with your request. Check *Writer's Market* for availability and cost.

Information concerning each publisher's specialization or special interest can be found in both *Literary Market Place* and *Writer's Market.*

Subject Guide To Books In Print and *Subject Guide To Forthcoming Books In Print*, both published by R. R. Bowker Co., are also excellent sources of information about publishers' specializations.

However, the fact that a publisher has published books on a certain subject does not necessarily mean he is interested in more books on that same subject. It may, in fact, mean just the opposite. For example, a publisher may currently have a book on breast cancer in his backlist or scheduled as a forthcoming release. A new submission on this same subject, no matter how well done, may be rejected as redundant, and competitive with the earlier work.

Submission Requirements

All publishers, no matter how large, have a budgeted number of books which they can effectively accept, publish, and finance each year. The number of professional staff members who are experienced and trained to handle the requirements is limited; the financing requirements for each new title accepted are high.

Every established publisher receives many unsolicited manuscripts from authors every week. It takes many, many hours to read and thoughtfully evaluate a book-length manuscript, and the cost is significant. Most publishers find that they must reject more than 100 manuscripts for every one they accept. A National Writers Club survey indicates that more than 100,000 unsolicited manuscripts are received annually—and less than one-half of one percent are ever published.

For all of these reasons publishers have found it necessary to restrict the onslaught of unsolicited manuscripts in some manner.

An increasingly large number of the more well-known publishers (Grosset, Harcourt Brace Jovanovich, Pocket Books, Simon and Schuster, and others) have elected to work only through literary agents. All publishers make every possible effort to communicate their needs, areas of specialization, policies, and restrictions to new authors through such trade publications as *Literary Market Place, Publisher's Weekly*, and *Writer's Market*. Still the flood of new manuscripts continue, and enormous amounts of time and effort are spent—and wasted—by authors and publishers alike.

Most publishers specify that authors initially submit query letters with outlines and sample chapters. While most new authors probably feel that neither a query nor an outline enable them to fairly present their work, editors can, in fact, make some important observations from such abbreviated submissions.

They can, for example, quickly determine whether the proposed material fits their publishing needs in general and especially at that particular point in time. Submissions involving subjects already in the publisher's backlist, or currently being produced, can be eliminated.

New authors, especially, are notorious for ignoring publishers' requirements, specializations, and needs. Novels are sent to textbook publishers, adventure books are sent to religious publishers, works of fiction are sent to publishers who consistently state that they publish nonfiction only. With queries, such misdirected submissions can be caught quickly and at minimum cost.

Every publisher develops, over a period of years, an intuitive sense for 'our kind of book.' It is not only a matter of subject but a matter of the author's approach and style.

While no publisher can afford to admit it, the fact is that their 'slush piles' of submissions are so overwhelming that they are literally forced to look for legitimate reasons to reject both queries and manuscripts. However exasperating this may be to the new writer who has poured his energy and dreams into his manuscript, it is a reality that must be faced. The only way to beat it is to learn to play the game by the rules.

Your single, overriding objective for your query must be to persuade the editor to accept and read your manuscript—all of it (if possible), not just the first few pages. Here are some rules that will help:

1. Your query letter should be perfect; beautifully typed, well-spaced, grammatically correct, and void of typing errors and misspelled words. It should not be too humble, too clever, or too cute. It should provide, in a straightforward, businesslike way, all of the relevant information needed by the editor to make an evaluation, including the proposed title, subject area, and kind of book. The story line or overview should be covered in about three sentences. A statement should be included to establish identifiable needs and potential markets. Excessively optimistic forecasts should be avoided. In fact, a position of understatement is usually wise.

   Since the query letter should be held to one page if at all possible, and seldom more than two, this is obviously a very difficult task. Authors often have more trouble explaining their book than they had writing it, so you may need some help. Unless you are an expert typist you will certainly want to use the services of someone who is. Remember that your letter of query *is* your book at this stage of the game. Rewrite your query as many times as necessary until it conveys exactly the right message in exactly the right tone.

If you include an outline, structure it like a table of contents. After each sectional heading give the main points covered in a very brief statement of short word summaries separated by dashes. (Rules and techniques for preparing your manuscript are given in a Chapter 4.)

2. Biographical data is important, especially if your work is nonfiction, since it allows the editor to determine your status and credibility as an expert in the field covered. A listing of stories and articles published or at press should be included, provided the publications have some stature. Book credits are very important. However, books published by subsidy publishers should be omitted.

All such information must be kept as brief and pertinent as possible, avoiding lists of meaningless credits. Do not include this data in the query letter itself; record it on a separate page which can accompany the query.

3. Always include a self-addressed, stamped envelope (SASE) when making a request of or submission to any publisher located in the United States. When contacting publishers in other countries include an International Reply Coupon, which can be purchased at the post office. Be sure enough postage is applied for the material involved and that the envelope provided is large enough to hold it.

This may seem unimportant, but it is a source of irritation with all publishers. The time, stationery, and postage involved in responding to queries and requests of various kinds make a real difference in a publisher's cost of operations. The omission of a SASE immediately labels the sender as an amateur who has not taken the trouble to do his homework. As a result, most publishers receiving unsolicited manuscripts without SASE will either discard them or immediately return them, unread.

4. Address your communication, by name if at all possible, to the editor in charge of the department concerned with

your kind of book (e.g., juvenile, textbook, etc.). This information is available from both *Writer's Market* and *Literary Market Place* for most major trade publishers. Be sure the name and title of the editor is accurate and is spelled correctly. When in doubt, verify by telephoning the publisher's switchboard operator.

If you are writing for a catalog or style sheet, identify the area of your request on the envelope so that it can be immediately routed to the proper department. Do not request catalogs or style sheets with your query. This material should have been obtained at a much earlier time.

5. If you are sending a photocopied submission which is not being submitted simultaneously to other publishers, attach a brief note providing assurance that this is the case.

6. Some authors use specially printed business letterheads for their queries. While this is not necessary, perhaps not even desirable, if you do so be certain that the letterhead is tastefully designed, professionally printed, and presents an acceptable image. Flashy letterheads, or those with caricatures, large type, or pretentious titles, do more harm than good.

7. Finally, know your publisher. Learn what he wants and how he wants it, and then follow his instructions to the letter. This information can be obtained directly from most publishers, in advance, by simply requesting their guidelines for authors. It is also available in a more abbreviated form in *Writer's Market* and *Literary Market Place*. Never query a publisher without having studied such instructions.

Simultaneous Submissions

Many publishers will accept simultaneous submissions, meaning that queries or manuscripts may be forwarded to other publishers at the same time you're sending theirs. Some publishers state that simultaneous submissions are 'OK if advised.' Still others want to know the track record of any manuscript they receive, and a few will not consider simultaneous submissions at all.

If the truth were known, no publisher likes simultaneous submissions. The cost of even perfunctory manuscript evaluation is so high, and so poor a gamble, that having to compete with an unknown number of other publishers brings the risk/investment factor to a nearly intolerable level. Yet, with rejection ratios of 100:1 or higher, it is inhumane to require single submissions, especially when reporting times usually run several weeks, or even months. If a writer doesn't make multiple submissions he could literally spend years finding a receptive publisher. When a manuscript is topical such delays can be disastrous.

Photocopied Submissions

Many publishers dislike photocopied submissions, and some will refuse to accept them. The reason usually given is that the type may be blurred and unreadable. With modern photocopying equipment, however, such objections are far less valid. The real reason that publishers don't like photocopied submissions is more likely to be that they imply simultaneous submissions.

However, in view of today's high costs of manuscript typing, especially when two or more carbons are required, the demand for typed originals is absurd. There is also the problem of telltale marks and folds on such originals which automatically inform second and third recipients that the manuscript has been previously rejected.

What should you do? Frankly, it's a gamble with no certain answer. Probably the best thing is to always query. Then, when your manuscript is requested, send your one typed original keeping an adequate supply of high quality photo copies for your files and, if necessary, for additional submissions.

Reporting Times

A new writer may spend years writing and polishing a manuscript. When he finally finishes the last page of the final draft it has usually become the most important single thing in his life—his offspring, his creation, his reason for being. And he wants it published—or at least read—now, today! It is as though the entire publishing world were waiting, quivering with anticipation, for its receipt.

The days, and finally the weeks, go by. And as each week passes, confusion turns to bewilderment, then to dismay, finally to anger. Was it misrouted, lost? Is it proceeding through endless readings, conferences, and impending judgments? Was the return address somehow omitted?

The answer is usually far simpler. The fact is that your precious manuscript has merely joined the flood of others that inundate overworked editors. The backlog is staggering.

Of 488 publishers studied, 129 promise replies in two months; 32 promise three months; and one—believe it or not—promises no more than eight months!

Rejections

By the time an unpublished author has received his third rejection notice, his psyche has taken a terrible beating. However effectively a new writer may be able to pump himself up—over and over again—trying to convince himself of the intrinsic value of his work; however loving, supportive, and confident the opinions of his family and friends, he never really knows, for sure, if he is 'right.' There is always that tiny doubt that maybe, just maybe, he is the one out of step; that what he perceives as reality and truth may, in fact, be only a mirage, a form of self-delusion. Such doubts, however camouflaged in certainty, can become overpowering.

Then, as the rejections begin to come—as they usually will, in the beginning—each one reinforces and nurtures that fertile seed of self-deprecation waiting to sprout.

The fact is, however, that most rejections have nothing whatsoever to do with your talent as a writer or the real value of your material. One well-known editor has stated that from one-half to two-thirds of the manuscripts rejected are rejected, out of hand, for purely mechanical or policy reasons. Here are a few:

1. The manuscript may be on a subject area that is outside the publisher's area of specialization and interest.
2. It may be on a subject that is already adequately covered in backlist or presently under contract for production.
3. The query or manuscript may be amateurishly prepared.
4. A self-addressed stamped envelope may not have been included.
5. The manuscript may be either too long or too short to fit the publisher's preferred format and standards for the type of book involved.
6. The timing may be bad. The publisher may have just received market research data suggesting that books in your subject area are showing a current decline in reader enthusiasm, while upswings are indicated in others.
7. The publisher's list for the coming period may be full and additional acceptances would exceed his budget and staff resources.
8. The publisher may feel that your credentials are not strong enough to adequately support a book on the subject covered.
9. One of the publisher's big-name authors may, by pure coincidence, have simultaneously submitted a 'blockbuster' which requires and deserves maximum possible effort and budget allowance, leaving little room for anything else.

There are many reasons for a manuscript being rejected, one of which may be that you do not have a salable product. But it can be a serious error to conclude this too quickly.

Rethink your project. Restudy your outline, your organization, your plot. Reread each paragraph, attempting to view your work dispassionately through the eyes of an editor who doesn't know you and is necessarily viewing your work solely in terms of potential sales and reader response. Re-evaluate the market need for your material and, once again, compare your book to those presently available on your subject. Ask friends and experts to give you their honest criticism.

If, after all this, you can again convince yourself of the value of your material, grit your teeth, bow your neck, and start again. Try the literary agents that specialize in your general area and kind of book. Especially try the smaller and more highly specialized publishers. You may even decide it would be worth the investment to pay for a professional evaluation of your manuscript. Many literary agents offer such services. *Writer's Digest* has a Writer's Digest Criticism Service which is highly reputable and was organized precisely for this common need.

The influence of plain, unvarnished luck cannot be over-looked, and it can work for you as well as against you. Somewhere along the line you may just happen to contact an editor who is faced with a gaping hole in his new seasonal listing which he badly needs to fill. Or you might come across that special editor with a personal interest in your particular subject and approach.

So keep on sending your work to publishers—and don't give up. Eventually you will probably receive an offer—and you will be on your way!

In the meantime, keep writing, keep working, and keep hoping. Only amateurs let rejection slips bring them to a dead halt as they anxiously await the next mail delivery.

Payments to Authors

Whatever other factors may motivate a writer to write, one measure of acceptance and success is money. Once the euphoria of first-publication has passed, it becomes a matter of professional pride and economic common sense to be certain that the compensation received is fair and at least equal to that being paid elsewhere for comparable results.

Unfortunately, judging what is 'fair' in today's economy and marketplace is almost impossible. In many ways writing is comparable to professional sports. The superstars can demand, and be willingly paid, millions of dollars for their services; other valuable, experienced, skilled, and loyal members of the same team—often doing the same job—may only receive a relative pittance. The difference lies in the ability to draw big crowds and to make the 'big play,' when it is needed. But efforts to justify the enormous differences are futile—it simply can't be done. It's largely a phenomenon of mass marketing and mass audiences, nurtured by television and motion pictures.

Mario Puzo, author of *The Godfather*, received over $500,000—after taxes and agents fee—for paperback reprint rights to *Fools Die* before the hardcover edition was even released. In the six year period from 1972 to 1978 Puzo made at least $6 million from his books and movies. Before *Godfather* his combined income from two earlier novels amounted to $6,500. (*Time*, August 28, 1978)

Lippincott bid over $400,000 for a story about the survivors of a plane crash and sold reprint rights for about $1 million before the book was ever written.

Jonathan Livingston Seagull, published by Macmillan, sold over six million copies. Reprint rights sold for $1.1 million. This phenomenal success was initiated almost entirely by word-of-mouth advertising.

The author of *Shogun*, James Clavell, received a $25,000 advance from Dell Publishing Company based solely on an outline.

In today's marketplace, when the right author writes the right book at the right time, all the 'rules' of compensation become meaningless. Millions of dollars in royalties and other forms of compensation await the author who, somehow, comes upon that magical formula that releases the genie of massive public acceptance. Whatever their formularized policies may suggest to the contrary, most publishers will pay whatever they must and are able to pay when they become convinced that such an opportunity is within their grasp.

It is important to understand, therefore, that any consideration of payments to authors applies only to the 'normal' author of the 'normal' book, and is subject to explosive variations. Even within such norms, variations in author compensation are often extraordinary.

The so-called 'standard royalty' arrangement for hardback books is 10 percent of the retail price on the first 5,000 copies sold; 12.5 percent the next 5,000; and 15 percent thereafter. On mass-market paperback books the standard royalty is 4 to 8 percent of the retail price of the first 150,000 copies sold.

However, the author's study of the royalty policies of 537 publishers suggests that less than 25 percent follow such industry standards.

Most royalty percentages quoted by publishers apply to the list price of the books sold, but this is not always the case. Some publishers base royalties on the 'net' price of the books sold—and the difference is significant. Depending on how the word 'net' is defined, this can mean the price after the booksellers' and jobbers' discounts have been deducted. Or it can mean the net amount of list price sales after all returns have been deducted. Assuming the former definition, the net sale price of a $10 book may be only $4 to $5, since resale discounts can amount to 50 to 60 percent. Therefore, a 10 percent net royalty may be the equivalent to a 4 or 5 percent royalty based on list price. Even when publishers sell their books by direct mail or through book clubs the term 'net' should be clarified since such direct selling expenses can easily amount to 35 to 50 percent of the list price values involved.

Book returns are another factor that affect an author's royalties. Every publisher experiences a certain amount of returns. Most publishers that sell through bookstores offer 100 percent returns privileges within a specified period of time (often twelve months). Publishers selling by direct mail or through book clubs also often offer generous returns arrangements.

Since authors' royalties are usually paid on sales after all returns are received and credited, the amount of these returns becomes a matter of some interest. Trade book publishers experience average returns of 17 percent of net sales, ranging from 21 percent on adult hardback books to 8 percent on juvenile books. Professional book publishers (technical and scientific, business and other professionals, and medical) experience a 15 percent return rate. Mass-market paperback publishers average a 33 percent return rate on rack-size books and about 18 percent on non-rack sized books. Book clubs experience a 19 percent return rate.

Not all publishers pay on a royalty basis. Some offer a flat fee or purchase method, often as an alternative choice and occasionally in conjunction with royalties. Announced fees usually range from a low of $50 to a high of $1,500. However, most publishers do not specify either minimums or maximums, leaving the amounts open to negotiation.

Advances are amounts paid to authors prior to publication of their manuscripts. As with royalties, they fluctuate dramatically, especially between successful authors with proven track records, big-name, first-time authors, and lesser-known authors. Advances are 'bets' by the publisher on how many books will be sold from the first printing, influenced by how badly that publisher needs to maintain a long-term, harmonious relationship with the author involved. When an author is a proven producer of profitable books, his publisher will usually do everything possible to relieve his financial anxieties and needs between books by maintaining a continuing flow of advances in anticipation of future manuscripts. One of the worst things that can happen to a really creative author (and to his publisher) is for him to be expending his energies worrying about paying the rent when he could be devoting those efforts to yet another best seller.

For lesser talents, however, advances are very much another matter. The risk the publisher takes by even agreeing to publish such books is very high. The additional risk of significant advances is simply too much for many publishers. When they do make advances, it is usually with great reluctance.

How important are royalty rates, fees, and advances to the author?

Royalty rates, considered alone, are almost meaningless. A 20 percent royalty from a publisher who has neither the means nor the ability to edit and produce that book professionally, or to market it successfully over the geographic area the subject demands, may be far less rewarding than a 10 percent, even a 5 percent, royalty from a publisher with such resources.

All things equal, however, compensation arrangements are matters of crucial importance to the established author. Such authors will naturally make every effort to negotiate the most favorable terms possible.

To the new or struggling author the problem is far more complicated. He is the 'seller'—and the publisher sits in the 'buyers' seat. He generally needs the publisher far more than the publisher needs (or recognizes the need for) another unknown author.

Then there is the problem of 'being published'—of credits. An author with several successful books to his credit will be in a far stronger position with his new books than an author who has never published a book at all. So there is the ever-present pressure to accept almost any arrangement, just to get published.

But there is another side. While a writer of magazine articles, short stories, etc. may feel that one article is only the precursor to hundreds of increasingly better ones to follow, books are another matter. How many *Roots* or *Gone With The Wind* can a single author hope to produce? Many extraordinary authors may have but one or two real masterpieces in them. If they, in effect, 'give them away,' under absurdly low financial arrangements, they may well lose forever their hope for really significant financial rewards. It happens.

The greatest potential for major financial rewards for authors and publishers alike, lies not with the original hardback publications but with subsidiary rights (reprint sales to mass-market paperback publishers, book clubs, television, motion pictures, foreign publishers, etc.). Fortunes are made through such sales. While considerable negotiating is usually involved, authors and original publishers often split income from reprint rights on a 50-50 basis. With other subsidiary rights, 70 to 90 percent may go to the author.

Literary Agents

Donald MacCampbell states that *90 percent of everything that is published commercially is handled by literary agents.* About 600 literary agents are listed in *Literary Market Place.*

The literary agent is primarily a sales agent, representing the interests of the authors whom he has under contract. He sells the products of his authors to book publishers, motion picture and television producers, theatrical producers, magazine publishers, and elsewhere. Most literary agents are located in or near New York City, but they are often also affiliated with agents located in California who specialize in motion picture and television rights, and with agencies in foreign countries.

Most literary agents charge their clients a 10 percent agency fee on all U.S. book sales; some charge 15 percent or even more. Commissions on short stories and magazine articles are often subject to flat minimum fees due to the time and relatively few dollars involved. Contracts with foreign publishers may require commissions of up to 20 percent since the foreign agencies also have to be compensated.

Some literary agencies are one-man operations, handling only a few authors; others have large staffs and may handle hundreds of authors. Some specialize (mass-market paperbacks, general fiction, etc.) while others will handle salable manuscripts of any kind.

Most agents, like most publishers, prefer to work with authors with established track records. But they also recognize that this is a dead-end policy which will undermine their futures. So, however reluctantly, they also continue to search for new talent to add to their 'stable.' Most new authors are found through recommendations from friends, publishers, editors, and literary scouts. A few are found through the hundreds of over-the-transom (unsolicited) manuscripts which they receive each year from new and unpublished authors.

At their best, literary agents provide an invaluable service to authors, publishers, and the industry as a whole. They are professionals—knowledgeable, conscientious, hard working, and reliable. They can be friends, supporters, and mentors to their authors, literally the difference between success and failure. They can easily double an author's exposure and income, due to their sophisticated savvy, expert judgment, and broad contacts within the industry. They are respected and valued by publishers who rely on their judgment and advice, thereby making their own jobs infinitely easier and less hazardous.

At their worst, they can be no better than confidence men who charge fees for work poorly or rarely done, who have the respect and confidence of none within the industry, and who lie in wait for that one, undeniable talent which they can ride to fame and fortune.

Subsidy Publishing

Subsidy publishing, also known as 'vanity' publishing, is a method of book publishing through which the risk/reward ratio is, theoretically, reversed. In trade publishing virtually all economic risks are borne by the publisher. If a book fails, the publisher loses money; when a book succeeds and becomes a best-selling bonanza, the publisher stands to make the lion's share of the profits. In subsidy publishing most or all of the economic risks are borne by the author, but if the book happens to succeed he is supposed to receive a major portion of the profits realized.

While this reversal of the risk/reward structure seems fair enough, provided the facts and conditions are accurately spelled out and understood in advance, subsidy publishing is generally held in low esteem within the book industry. The following quote from *The Writing Business*, by Donald MacCampbell, is representative of the general attitude:

"Librarians as well as reviewers and booksellers shy away from subsidized books. . . . It is highly doubtful that those involved in the dissemination of books will ever overcome their deep-seated aversion to subsidized publishing. . . . I am often shown books put out by vanity publishers. Both books and the covering letters go immediately *into the trash.*"

While others within the industry are rarely so candid, it is overwhelmingly evident that many share similar views. The question is, why?

Many of the problems of subsidy publishing are realistically explored in an article titled "Does It Pay To Pay To Have It Published?" which originally appeared in the January, 1975 *Writer's Digest.* (Free reprints are available by sending a self-addressed, stamped envelope to Payin' For It Editor, *Writer's Digest,* 1507 Dana Ave, Cincinnati, OH 45207.) This article includes 22 specific questions which should be answered before signing a subsidy contract. Every writer considering this method of publishing should read it.

There is little doubt that the history of vanity publishing has been less than distinguished. Like most industries catering to the dreams of fame and fortune by inexperienced hopefuls, it has had more than its share of confidence men, unscrupulous promoters, and out-and-out crooks. Yet, the fact that some subsidy publishers have survived and prospered for 50 years, that thousands of books are published under such contracts every year, that many of the authors involved are apparently content, and that the business is growing, all seem to suggest that at least some legitimate needs are being met.

Many of the unethical practices of vanity publishers have been curbed in recent years by rulings and indictments by the Federal Trade Commission. Most of the companies involved have become more cautious about the promises they make.

The real problem, however, is inherent in the process itself. In trade publishing about 99 percent of all manuscripts and queries submitted are rejected. Whatever the reasons may be, and no matter the occasional error and injustice, the fact remains that a very high level of selectivity exists which inevitably means a higher quality level of books being published (or at least books that are more readable and more marketable).

In subsidy publishing, where the publisher bears little or no risk, at least 99 percent of all manuscripts submitted are accepted for publication.

An analogy can be made to the selection procedures of colleges and universities. The higher the admission standards, the higher the academic caliber of the eventual graduates. The general relationship is inescapable. (But, as with less competitive colleges, occasional literary giants sometimes defy the averages. This can also happen in subsidy publishing.)

A second weakness of subsidy publishing lies in the caliber of the creative editing provided. While the mechanical aspects of editing—copy editing for grammar, spelling, and punctuation, and production editing for the printer—involve skills that are usually available at reasonable costs, creative editing is not. Creative editors are talented artists in their own right; they are scarce and in high demand. They usually take a great deal of pride in both their authors and the results of their mutual efforts toward a common goal—the finest, most salable, most readable book possible for the objectives involved.

While all authors need and can benefit greatly from such editorial support—even that small group of experienced, professional writers—none need it more desperately than those dealing with subsidy publishers, writers that are usually amateurs or semi-professionals. Since high caliber creative editing is rarely available from subsidy publishers, most manuscripts receive only mechanical forms of editing. The results, as *Writer's Digest* so aptly describes, are often 'wooden' books which somehow seem to miss their mark.

A third weakness lies in the area of marketing. While all reputable subsidy publishers make *some* effort at marketing, it is usually confined to the more mechanistic avenues that are equally available to everyone. Books are listed in *Books In Print* and other reference guides; a certain number of review copies are routinely circulated; the book is included in the subsidy publisher's catalog; mail announcements are made to larger bookstores and libraries, and ads—usually multiple-book ads—are sometimes placed in a few publications. But, due largely to the 'aversion' of the industry, the more credible forms of publicity are largely denied to subsidy publishers.

While the foregoing comments may seem to be a devastating indictment, there are positive aspects.

There are many excellent books written that are addressed to such a limited audience or on such esoteric or personal subjects that it would be economically impossible for them to ever yield an acceptable profit to a trade publisher. (A trade publisher must usually sell 7,500 to 10,000 copies of a book on a first printing just to break even.) This is the reason university presses subsidize many of the books that they publish, either directly, through appropriations and grants, or indirectly, through budgeted losses. If this were not done a large number of books of academic merit could never be published.

Many books are written for limited markets. They include regional, local, and family histories, genealogies, corporate biographies, short stories and poetry, personal books with religious or philosophical implications, and others.

The writers of such books rarely aspire to high literary status—that is not their objective. Nor do their readers necessarily demand it. Yet, their books are often valued and important to the audience for which they are intended. And the cost of putting their material into permanent and attractive book form is (or should be) less than duplicating and binding an equal number of copies for the same audience.

After all, an amateur artist, who has no intention of turning professional, at least has the joy of his art and the fulfillment of sharing it with friends and loved ones. An amateur or semi-professional musician can share his music. But the writer, surely their equal in artistry and creativity, has nothing to share until his writings are reproduced onto the printed page.

One cannot help but suspect that at least some of the stormy resentment to subsidy publishing is a kind of literary elitism. Many 'name' publishers engage in subsidy publishing to varying degrees, though few openly admit it. Of 571 trade publishers studied, seventy-one admit to varying degrees of subsidy publishing; the actual total is undoubtedly much higher. For example, *My Years With General Motors*, by Alfred P. Sloan, Jr., which was published by McGraw-Hill and is reported to have been subsidized, turned out to be a great financial success. Many trade publishers have now established special departments to handle subsidized books and one large paperback house has a special imprint for subsidized projects.

It is incorrect and unfair to generalize, as some do, that all subsidy publishing is 'bad.' It obviously has its place. However, it should be approached with caution and without illusions. If you cannot afford the loss of the investment involved, stay away from it.

Charges to authors have been known to run as high as $15,000—no small investment—and the probability of recovering more than 25 percent of that investment is very low. Especially questionable is the practice of holding title to all books published in the name of the publisher, with the author never actually owning the books that he pays for.

Whether a far lower and far more controllable investment in self-publishing, involving total ownership of all books produced, full title to all profits, and maximum author participation, would be wiser is a decision which only the author can make.

The Author/Publisher Contract

It is important that every reasonable source of potential misunderstanding between author and publisher be anticipated and resolved in advance. While every relationship is different —especially in regard to marketing responsibilities and whether a trade or subsidized agreement is contemplated — the following points should be considered:

1. The author should grant to the publisher the right to print, publish, and sell the book, in specified languages,

for the full term of the copyright—including renewals and extensions.

2. The publisher's rights should cover: paperback or hardback reprints; sale through book clubs in complete, condensed, or abridged versions; condensations and abridgements; magazines and newspapers; anthologies, compilations, and digests; quotations in other works; Braille versions; use in information storage and retrieval systems, in all existing and future technologies.

3. Additional subsidiary rights should cover: dramatic, musical, public reading, radio, television, motion pictures, and allied rights; translations; adaptations for commercial and promotional activities.

4. The geographical areas covered by such rights, whether exclusive or non-exclusive, should be specified.

5. Rights not specifically granted should be reserved to the author.

6. The author must not cause to be published any version of the work which adversely effects the publisher's rights.

7. The author should warrant that: work is original and not in the public domain; that the author is sole author with full power to assign rights; that work has not been previously published; that there is no infringement of proprietary rights, statutory copyrights, or other rights; that work contains no obscene, libelous, or unlawful material; that statements are true and based on reasonable research; that biographical work is 'as told to the author'; that the author will not assign publisher's rights.

8. The author should indemnify and hold publisher harmless from claims or damages instituted by reason of publication, sale, or distribution of work.

9. The author should agree to deliver two copies of the completed manuscript, in English, to the publisher in final form with illustrations and other required materials ready-for-production.

10. The publisher must be allowed to make necessary editorial changes to the author's manuscript.

11. The obligation for the expense of publication must be specified, including the time frame, and the author's remedies if publication is not made.

12. The responsibility for registration of the copyright, and in whose name, must be set forth—including provisions for its renewal.

13. The publisher must agree to furnish galley proofs to the author, and the author must agree to proofread, correct, and return proofs within specified times. Responsibility for payment of excessive author's alterations (usually beyond 10 percent of typesetting costs) must be set forth.

14. Royalty payments that the author will receive, and whether on net or list price values, must be specified for both hardback and paperback editions—both in varying quantities. Provisions for sharing income from reprint sales and all other subsidiary sales must be made. Provisions should be made for copies sold for export and at special prices, such as to book clubs and organizations outside of regular book selling channels; copies destroyed, given away, or sold below cost; and on overstocks and damaged copies.

15. Royalty percentages should be specified on all other granted rights.

16. Dates on which royalty statements and payments to the author by the publisher are due must be specified, with provisions for reserves against returns, deductions for overpayments, and other charges or advances to the author's account, and claims against the publisher resulting from author's representations or warranties.

17. The number of free copies to which the author is entitled, and the price to be paid for additional copies for the author's personal use, should be specified.

18. Provision should be made for the termination of the agreement when the work goes out of print, or when the publisher fails to reprint, including the disposition of existing stocks—except in circumstances beyond the publisher's control. A definition of 'out of print' should be established.

19. The publisher must be authorized to institute legal action against copyright infringement, or unauthorized use of the work, and the distribution to be made of monies recovered should be indicated.
20. If the agreement is terminated, all licenses and other grants of rights to other parties must survive and remain valid.
21. The state laws under which the agreement is made should be specified.
22. Provision should be made for future modification or waiver of the agreement; assignment of the agreement; use of author's name, likeness, and biographical material.

The comment is occasionally heard from new and small publishers that 'our contract consists of about five lines'—the implication being that this is a tribute to their honesty and a measure of their authors' trust. And, often, such gentlemen's agreements are adequate.

But we live in a complex world filled with enormous diversities in values. What is true and fair to one is frequently the opposite to another. Also, the pressures created by massive economic inducements can sometimes be overwhelming to even erstwhile saints.

So, beware! Beware of those charming charlatans who wave the magic wand of their charisma and tell you that a comprehensive agreement is really not necessary, for it could be the only real security you have.

Chapter 2

Self-Publishing

When an author self-publishes he assumes the dual role of *author* and *publisher*. He pays all costs, receives all profits, and is personally responsible for the final success of his own book.

Self-publishing is one of the fastest growing segments of today's book industry. What was once a defensive, last-ditch alternative, brought on by endless rejections from trade publishers has now become a positive first choice for many authors, with an increasingly attractive record of success— financial and personal. Here are some of the reasons for the change:

1. New developments in book production equipment now make it possible to produce high quality books in small quantities at competitive unit costs. Many small book typesetters and book printers around the country are now offering the specialized services required.

2. The 'mysteries' of book publishing, especially in the area of marketing, have been thoroughly explored in recent years in books such as this one. The avenues of free

publicity, which are available to publishers of all sizes, are now well known to most authors.

3. The national trend to direct mail marketing for books, which now accounts for more than 25 percent of all book orders, has made small self-publishers less dependent on traditional book marketing channels.

4. Inflation, extra leisure time, the do-it-yourself movement, personal and family problems, etc. have all combined to create a steadily rising demand for self-help, how-to, and other nonfiction books written by experts from every field imaginable. These types of books are extraordinarily compatible with the strengths inherent in self-publishing.

5. The seemingly elitist and esoteric attitudes of some northeastern publishers—brought on, in reality, by the basic law of supply and demand—have caused large numbers of highly qualified authors to seek other options. Self-publishing has developed into a viable alternative.

6. The unusually high gross profit umbrella traditional in the book industry is now understood by most authors. Those with economic savvy can readily compute the enormous profit possibilities which can be realized when a book becomes a real seller.

There was a time when most new authors believed that the prestige of having a big publisher's name on their books was at least as important as any economic rewards which they might receive. Merely being able to tell friends and associates that one's book had been 'accepted' suddenly made one a 'writer,' whether the book sold well or not.

Many writers still feel this way. The euphoria of acceptance can be more meaningful than all other considerations combined.

The New Writer

Today, a new breed of writer is emerging. He has no dreamy literary ambitions, for he is usually already successful and acknowledged within his area of expertise. He is sophisticated enough to know that 'being accepted' by a national publisher is not really an end but a beginning, and that much of what happens next will, in any case, be up to him (talk show appearances, autograph parties, personal tours, etc.).

Frequently his reasons for writing a book in the first place include the achievement of certain objectives which may or may not involve the book itself. Finally, he understands—as a professional and expert himself—that a successful book can be a real money-maker (with many legitimate tax saving possibilities), and can be challenging, stimulating, and great fun in the bargain.

No retiring poets or frustrated novelists here. Such writers are tough, capable, knowledgeable achievers who know— even better than many publishers—how to get the most from each dollar invested.

Most self-publishers, while not professional writers, are experienced, seasoned experts in their chosen field—who have something worthwhile to pass on to the rest of us. Having something of real value to say is, after all, what books and writing are really all about. *Without it they are fluff.*

Our world is changing. New technologies, procedures, and solutions are being developed regularly. It is difficult for most of us to even keep up, much less stay ahead. We have entered an era in which every skilled, trained individual must invest a substantial portion of his time in continuing education or be left behind.

People everywhere hunger to know. They want to improve, learn new skills, better their standard of living, advance in their jobs and professions, expand their minds and their understanding.

They want to learn new crafts, find new hobbies, develop new avocations which will provide meaning and interest to that portion of their lives that extends beyond working and sleeping. They want to improve their social and business relationships, their marital relationships, their family relationships. They want solid, worthwhile help in finding personal fulfillment and, hopefully, some measure of happiness, contentment, and self-satisfaction.

But they will only accept such help and advice from those who truly know. Who better to author such books than the proven experts within each area of interest? The opportunities are extraordinary for those who are determined to remain at the forefront of their disciplines and areas of expertise.

Authors who can fill such needs will find many rewards.

First, an important social need is being served.

Second, the adage that 'the teacher learns more than the student' is especially true in the authorship of books. No matter how skilled and experienced an author may be, when he attempts to organize and articulate that knowledge into manuscript form, he inevitably involves himself in a new and enlarging learning experience.

A third fortunate result is the fact that writing a book automatically enhances that writer's reputation and credibility. However successful and respected he may have been before, he will now be elevated to an even higher level, once his book is in print .

The Self-Publishing Tradition

Whatever the reasons for self-publishing a book, there is a long and distinguished tradition to support the decision. Here are just a few of the many prominent authors who financed one or more of their own books:

Thomas Gray	*Elegy*
Edward Fitzgerald	*The Rubaiyat of Omar Khayyam* (translation)
Leo Tolstoy	*War and Peace*
A. E. Housman	*A Shropshire Lad*
Marcel Proust	*Remembrance of Things Past*
Mary Baker Eddy	*Science & Health & the Key to the Scriptures*
Henry Martyn	*Robert's Rules of Order*
Thomas Hardy	*Desperate Remedies*
Henry Thoreau	*Walden*
John Bartlett	*Familiar Quotations*
William Strunk, Jr.	*The Elements of Style*
Eugene O'Neill	*Thirst*

Other famous authors who self-published their own books include: Nathaniel Hawthorne, Elizabeth Barrett Browning, Alexander Pope, George Gordon, Lord Byron, Percy Bysshe Shelley, Alfred Lord Tennyson, Stephen Crane, Edwin Arlington, Willa Cather, James M. Barrie, Walt Whitman, Vachel Lindsay, Ezra Pound, T. S. Eliot, Rudyard Kipling, Rod McKuen, Robert Browning, Edgar Rice Burroughs, Edgar Allan Poe, George Bernard Shaw, Ernest Hemingway, Sir John Masefield, Fanny Farmer, and Mark Twain.

Here are a few of the thousands of famous authors who have had their work rejected by one or more trade publishers: Thomas Paine (*Common Sense*), Lloyd C. Douglas (*Magnificent Obsession*), Upton Sinclair (*The Jungle*), Arnold Bennett (*Old Wive's Tales*), William Shirer (*Rise and Fall of the Third Reich*), James Joyce, Sinclair Lewis, Theodore Dreiser, and William Faulkner.

Kyle Onstott, a sixty-nine year old Californian, wrote a book titled *Mandingo*. It was repeatedly rejected by New York publishers and finally self-published by the author. Over *three million copies were sold* in hardcover. Fawcett later reprinted the book and sold another five million copies.

Robert Ringer, author of *Winning Through Intimidation*, had his book turned down by ten publishers. He finally published it himself, with ads in the national media and with Funk & Wagnalls handling the distribution. Acting as his own agent, his book sold 1.7 million copies between 1973 and 1977.

Self-Publishers I Have Known

In terms of size, my own book printing and publishing firm is not large. Yet, we produce about 200 titles annually—many of which are for self-publishers.

Having worked with hundreds of authors over the years, I have developed a deep admiration and respect for them, both individually and as a group. While every successful self-publisher I have known is uniquely individual, they do, almost invariably, share certain common qualities. They are leaders and achievers filled with energy and drive, and an indomitable enthusiasm for the possible. They are very extraordinary human beings.

While it is impossible to completely categorize the books they write, here are a few examples:

Patient Information Books. One client of mine, a plastic surgeon, developed a small book containing information he wanted to communicate to new patients. It included detailed explanations of most basic operations, with 'before' and 'after' photographs for each. He gives them to new patients, saving himself enormous amounts of time and his patients significant amounts of money in pre-consultation fees. Now he can concentrate his time on the special and more advanced concerns of each patient, knowing that a foundation of knowledge has already been established.

He is currently in his third printing and has now produced a Spanish-language edition for patients from South America. (It is worth noting that his patient load doubled within six months of first publication.)

Another client, a pediatrician, wrote a hilarious, yet highly professional, little book titled *How To Raise The Perfect Child—Or The Impossible Dream.* It explained, in reassuring ways, those actions and reactions which are perfectly normal for young children, but which can create much anxiety for new mothers. He also discussed other symptoms and warnings which require prompt action. Finally, he provided a calendar for mothers that extended through the adolescent years of the child's life, showing the various shots, check-ups, and other health-related actions that need to be remembered.

While his objectives were the same as my plastic surgeon friend—to provide helpful information to his own patients— the book was so marvelous that it burst its original boundaries. It was soon being carried by practically every department store, baby store, and pharmacy in the area and became a real success story. Over 100,000 copies were sold, and his practice went wild with the rush of new patients.

A third client—a doctor of internal medicine—wrote an extraordinary book on autobiofeedback, also for his own patients. But somehow the word got out, and orders began coming in from every state in the union.

With medical care cost continuing to rise, and the physician's time being critically reduced, patient information books can serve an important function for doctor and patient alike. (There are also some interesting tax-savings possibilities, such as assigning future income from those books to low-income dependents through an inter vivos reversionary trust fund arrangement.)

'How-to' Success Books. A tall, high-powered Texan with a slow, southern drawl wandered into my office one day with a story of how he and his wife had made a million dollars selling undeveloped real estate. Though he had never written a book before—and probably not much else—he had put his success story onto paper and wanted to publish it in book form.

And he did!

After less than a year his book was in its fifth printing, had sold 75,000 copies to buyers throughout the U.S., and had become the foundation for a profitable national consulting service to individuals wanting to enter the field of land sales.

Home Improvement Books. I was recently approached by a retired engineer who had made a study of potential energy saving techniques in home construction. He had put it all together in a well-written, authoritative book titled *How To Build—Or Remodel—Your Energy Saving Home.*

By publication date he had orders from banks, lighting and power associations, and schools from all over the country. His books were soon stacked high (and selling briskly) in major bookstore throughout the area. Orders flooded in from all over the country, and even from foreign countries. After only six months he was already in his third printing, and had barely scratched the surface of his potential markets.

Cookbooks. Religious and other non-profit organizations are regularly faced with the problem of raising money, and cookbooks are an ideal way of doing so. I never cease to marvel at how many organizations continue to print—and make money—from them. Some time ago we produced 10,000 really splendid cookbooks for one church group. They sold out within six months.

I must say, though, that they approached their project like real 'pros.' Every recipe was pre-tested by three different groups. And they put so much friendly persuasion on the two leading area newspapers that they received, free of charge, full-page, four-color reviews in the Women's Section of each paper.

* * *

However, not all self-published books are written primarily to make money. In fact, some of the finest books we produce are essentially non-commercial:

Personal Philosophies. Several years ago I was contacted by a lovely little lady of eighty-five who wanted to publish some of her personal philosophies, essays, articles, and poems, mainly for her family and friends. In earlier years she had written columns and articles for several newspapers in the area.

Being more conservative than the situation probably warranted, I tried to gently discourage her in the project, knowing full well she could never recover her investment. But she persisted, and somehow in the process my price kept lowering, finally ending up somewhere below my cost. (I'm still not sure how this economic regression came about. I suspect that *I* may have been the *real* innocent.)

At any rate, her book was published, and she, her family, and her friends were ecstatic. During the long proofreading process, I became one of her fans. Many of her *Ironing Board Philosophies* still ring true and clear in my heart, and I shall never forget her. Many others, I suspect, feel the same.

Business Histories. With anti-business sentiment and lack of understanding widespread, it surely behooves forward-looking business leaders to present their philosophies and achievements as persuasively as possible to all who will listen, especially to present and future employees. A well-done, insightful corporate history is a wonderfully effective way to do just that. It provides a platform for in-depth considerations of obstacles and hopes that can be conveyed in no other way. It can help build company spirit, employee understanding, and a feeling of 'belonging' and being a part of a living, building tradition. It can present a side of its guiding executives that may otherwise remain hidden and it can help the community (even the powers in government) to better understand the negative influences of the artificial barriers being placed in its path. A broader support base can be developed from it; changes can be made.

With the thousands of customers, vendors, lenders, employees, and competitors that most such companies have, success in such a venture is almost automatic. (Taking my own advice, I recently wrote and published a history of our own company titled *A Printer's Story*.)

True Life Stories. A bouncy, energetic fellow of fifty-four approached me some years ago with a manuscript that had been turned down by several trade publishers. It was the story of his recovery from lung cancer five and one-half years earlier. He asked me to read it, and I did—*three times*.

How can I explain it? Can you imagine combining hilarious humor with the agony, pain, and threat of death from having a lung removed? Well, that's exactly what he did. As I read, my eyes would brim with tears one minute, and I would burst out laughing the next. How strange!

The author became a celebrity in the best Good Samaritan tradition. He regularly visited cancer clinics throughout the state, talking to and cheering despondent victims who saw nothing left to live for (as well as their distraught families), and gave away paperback copies of his book to those who couldn't afford to buy them. No sooner was someone struck with cancer than he was there, with convincing words of encouragement, hope, and practical advice. He became an inspiration to all who knew him, and especially to me.

A Personal Note: I wrote my own first book, *A Father's Legacy*, during the trying era of the early 60s. I wrote it for my children. In it I tried to discover and explain what I really believed about the many problems of the times and life in general. As so often happens, however, I was the one to be enlightened. Whatever my book may have done for others, it had a major impact on my own values and on the direction of my own life.

This book was followed, a little later, with *Insight: Foundation for College & Career*. Being more or less an extension of the first book, it was also oriented to what I perceived to be the needs of my own family. Still later I wrote a book titled *American Perspectives*—mainly, I think, for my own edification—in which I attempted to find some rational consensus for the philosophical polarizations that surround us.

None of these books were written for profit. And, while a modest readership has developed—largely through word-of-mouth—I have never attempted to market them commercially.

While subsequent books have been relatively profitable and are far more commercially acceptable (my college and career guide series has been used by many high school and college counselors and my book on small business management has been used as a university text), *none are as dear to me as these three.*

* * *

There are many reasons for self-publishing a book. *There are also reasons not to.*

If you are investing money which you need for other family purposes—your children's education, a new home, to pay your bills, etc.—*don't do it!*

If your investment will destroy your savings and place your family in a difficult financial position, *don't do it!*

If you must borrow the money and count on your book becoming a financial success to repay the loan, *don't do it!*

But if you *can* afford the investment of time and money, and *if you have something to say that's truly worth saying*, I sincerely recommend the experience. (I must believe in it—I have now written and self-published ten books of my own, plus innumerable manuals, booklets, and articles.)

The Book Printer

During the past thirty years, and especially within the past decade, the printing industry has become increasingly separated into many industries, each highly specialized and offering different services than the rest. Today there are business forms specialists, business card specialists, wedding announcement specialists, label manufacturers, carton printers, process color printers, quick copy printers, and many more. Each uses special equipment developed especially for that industry, special production techniques, and demands different skill combinations from its employees.

While this trend has been generally healthy for the trade and printing users alike, it *has* created problems in selecting the 'best' printer for a particular kind of job. It's not at all uncommon to find many hundreds of companies listed under 'Printers' in the Yellow Pages of a large metropolitan city. Yet *none are equally qualified or equipped in all areas of printing.*

While almost any printer can, theoretically, print books, a professional book printer is a *manufacturer*, usually specializing exclusively in books. To the uninitiated, the difference may seem obscure and insignificant, but it is enormous.

Specializing as he does, the book printer can develop—even in a relatively small plant—systems, techniques, and production flows which will allow dozens, even hundreds, of titles to move smoothly through his plant simultaneously, without confusion, bottlenecks, or delayed completion dates. If he does his own typesetting, his crew will be intimately familiar with the complex requirements of book typography and will be comfortable with the efficient, accurate output of massive amounts of typesetting that must be produced with maximum accuracy at minimum cost. He will provide specially designed pagination systems which reduce design time, errors and cost, substantially speed up pagination, and fit smoothly into the production activities that follow. His cameras, platemakers, and presses will all be oriented to the optimum sizes and special requirements of 'his kind of book.' If he does his own binding, he can eliminate all unrelated equipment facilities and problems (i.e., perforators, padding racks, snap-out forms equipment, etc.) and concentrate instead on the comparatively few, large, automated systems needed for book bindery.

A major advantage for the book printer lies in the

composition and depth of his paper inventories. Unlike the large job printer who must stock hundreds of kinds, colors, sizes, and finishes of paper, the book printer is able to concentrate his investment in relatively few kinds of book and cover papers. This not only reduces the possibility of shortages and the necessity of buying through local wholesalers, as most job printers do, but it also enables him to deal with a minimum number of paper mills, ordering in large quantities many months in advance at the lowest possible cost.

But book printers themselves vary, each concentrating on a special segment of the industry. Some will specialize in relatively short-run books, standardizing on many relatively small, flat sheet presses with fast single-operator make-ready and plate change capabilities. Others will pursue markets which regularly involve larger quantities, for which they may use large flat sheet perfecting presses (printing two sides simultaneously). Still others will serve the mass-market paperback publishers, using very large and expensive high-speed web presses (printing from rolls) which, while restricting book size, design, and paper selections, significantly reduce unit costs on the very long runs required. Today there are also 'Cameron Belt Presses' which, while having many limitations, reduce costs even further on books that meet their production requirements.

Each approach serves a special market in an especially acceptable manner. The problem for the author/publisher is to determine *which is which*.

Most successful book printers learn—often the hard way—not to mislead potential clients about their capabilities and facilities. There are few things that will bog down a manufacturer more quickly than to accept kinds of work that he is not geared to produce efficiently. Every book printer has his own special markets and area of expertise, and his entire plant will usually be focused sharply in that direction.

Ask, in specific terms, what that direction is. He will usually give you a definitive answer upon which you can base your evaluation. If not, review his sample room and ask to see his plant. Question the run quantities and markets involved for the various samples displayed. Check the sizes of his presses. Talk to his clients. You will soon develop a clear picture of his facilities and capabilities.

Most book printers restrict their responsibilities to typesetting, printing, and binding. (Many of the larger book manufacturers even prefer to work only from camera-ready copy, leaving the typesetting to others.) They do not, usually, involve themselves in editing, marketing, or fulfillment (e.g., shipping and billing) of orders for individual books.

As manufacturers, they do not, in theory at least, know or care (within legal and ethical limits) what a book says, how it is written, or who, if anyone, will ever buy it. They work to pre-established specifications, produce a quality book, and are paid for services rendered on the basis of firm, advance estimates. They neither speculate nor share in the potential profits or losses of the books they produce. When production is completed and the order is shipped, their responsibility ends—which leaves a big void for the self-publisher to fill—somehow.

Self-publishers dealing with traditional book printers will usually need additional help in three areas: editing, design, and marketing.

Free-lance specialists, with the technical background to copy edit a manuscript, are available in every major city. Many can mark a manuscript for a typesetter. The problem is to find them.

The book printer can often help with contacts he has in the industry. The English departments of the senior colleges and universities are a good source. They often have competent graduate or post-graduate students available or can recommend previous graduates. A newspaper classified ad sometimes brings good results. The local newspaper's book section editors can be helpful, as can bookstore owners and librarians. *Writer's Digest* often carries ads for free-lance editors.

The greatest difficulty usually lies in finding someone to help in creative editing: rewrites, additions and deletions, tightening, organization, and market-oriented advice.

Help is often also needed in the area of book design, especially cover and dust jacket design. Many of these same sources can provide leads in this area. Commercial art schools and college art departments can sometimes help. Local magazine publishers often use free-lance artists of the kind needed. The difficulty lies in finding artists who are oriented to commercial book art as opposed to other art forms, such as fashion art.

The marketing problem is big and complex, and there is no simple solution. If the right kind of small, aggressive advertising agency can be found, and they can be persuaded to take a real interest in the future of your book, they can be extremely helpful. Many larger cities have innovative and progressive direct mail advertising firms who know their business and the market. Most areas have regional bookseller organizations which can provide valuable advice in the marketing area.

In spite of all this, developing a competent support staff for a single book effort is difficult, and it involves a great deal of time, and trial and error, for the author/publisher.

The Book Specialist

A new kind of organization is evolving in a few major cities which may be called the book specialist. The principal is usually a book printer who truly loves books, and deeply believes in their importance, as well as the importance of their authors. While carrying out all of the traditional functions of the book printer, in the established, non-speculative manner, such firms extend their responsibilities to embrace the full range of services required by the self-publisher: editing, art work, marketing, and fulfillment. All services are provided at a charge, but you may use as many or as few as you choose, to whatever degree you specify. While it is possible—though not likely—that the charges involved may not be significantly less than you might be able to negotiate on your own, the difference lies in the degree of skill, responsibility, and interest that the book specialist's team can bring to your book. Since his staff—some in-plant and others free-lance—develops a team expertise from having worked together on many books, proving themselves on each, expensive and frustrating trial and error can be substantially reduced.

A Word on Price

There is no book printer or book specialist who cannot, on any given job, be beaten on price by some other printer who chooses to 'buy' the job. This is especially true when the low price originates from a firm which has no experience with the requirements and ramifications of professional book production, and may not even know what its true costs are.

When the production of a book is purchased on the basis of low price alone you will usually receive exactly what you pay for—rarely more. So, beware of such low prices from those without experience, facilities, and resources. They often result in a costly and heartbreaking experience. Especially beware of those without the skill and taste to understand and appreciate what a book is, how it should look, and what it should accomplish.

While it is true that an experienced and skilled book printer should, by the nature of his operation, enjoy production costs that are lower than his less-specialized competitors, he will usually not pass on all such savings to his clients—nor should he. Instead, if he is wise, he will invest them in people and equipment, to the long-range benefit of his clients. He will employ skilled proofreaders and conscientious inspectors to be certain that the books he produces are perfect. He will pay his production personnel wages and benefits that encourage them to stay with his firm for many years, providing clients with the full storehouse of their knowledge and experience. He will continually upgrade his equipment and facilities to provide the best that is available through modern technology. He will attract and retain skilled, creative, and caring executives and service personnel dedicated to serving the real needs of his clients—quality books that succeed in their objectives.

The saving of a few hundred dollars, in comparison to such dedication and professionalism, is false economy of the worst kind. Do not skimp on quality. There is no profit—or satisfaction—from amateurism in self-publishing.

Cost Considerations

There are two kinds of costs in book production: one-time costs and continuing costs. It is important that they be recognized and considered separately.

One-time costs involve those activities that are necessary for a book's original manufacture but, once completed, will not be incurred again (assuming that the design and content of the book remain unchanged). They include: artwork, editing, typesetting, pagination, and—in offset printing—negatives.

The cost of design and artwork can be very high (many thousands of dollars) or relatively modest, depending on what is needed and how it is achieved. An attractive inside page design is relatively easy to achieve, especially if you are dealing with an experienced book specialist with a wide selection of attractive, standing page formats from which to choose.

An attractive cover and dust jacket design that will really make the book stand out among other books, and sell it, is essential. Dull, drab books are dead before they start—regardless of their content. You may not be able to 'tell a book by its cover,' but covers still sell books. If you don't believe it, ask any bookstore owner or spend some time studying the cover designs on the mass-market paperback racks. They have to sell, and they do.

The problem, of course, is economics. A self-publisher with a market potential of 2,000 to 5,000 books and a limited budget can rarely afford to spend $5,000 for artwork. Even an investment of $1,000 can increase first-run costs by $.20 to $.50 per book. While this may not seem like much, when it is translated into list price requirements, at ratios of six or eight to one, it becomes very significant.

If you happen to have some talent in commercial art—or have a friend with such talent, you can save a great deal of money—but be careful. Many amateur artists turn out equally amateurish art, and you cannot afford to have that kind of design on your book. Designing books may seem simple, but it isn't. It is a special and demanding art form.

Good cover designs can frequently be composed largely of dramatic typography, printed in two or three ink colors. Such an approach can be relatively inexpensive. Unusual, carefully selected black-and-white photographs can often serve as background for a good cover design. This is also inexpensive.

One workable technique is to find three or four effective designs on published books that fit your general style and subject. You can, with some talent, reduce them to their basic structural elements (colors, balance, reverses, typographic style, etc.) and then translate them into the presentation you need for your own cover. While this may appear to be 'copying,' you will usually find that the process stimulates your own imagination and that the final translation will take on a look and feel of its own. Our company maintains a library of clip art books which we make available to clients at no charge. With a modicum of imagination, some striking and effective designs can be developed from their use.

Whatever technique you use, the final look must be 'right' and professional. Nothing less will do. While, at the very least, the added cost will probably be several hundred dollars, you can take some consolation in the fact that it is a one-time investment which will soon be forgotten if your book really sells.

Typesetting is usually the single largest item of one-time cost. Whatever typesetting method is used, cost is mainly a factor of keystrokes and complexity.

When a book typesetter estimates typesetting costs, he computes the total number of keystrokes involved, based on the original manuscript. Everything counts: punctuation, spaces, everything. He will then multiply the total character count equivalent for the text portion of the manuscript by a unit dollar per thousand price which he has developed from an on-going analysis of his production cost records. Front material, back material, tables, running heads, captions, etc., are estimated separately.

Most book typesetters will use at least five different pricing levels, which are primarily based on the complexity of the work and the average characters per hour of productivity that can be anticipated from typesetting operators. The typesetting requirements for a typical novel are usually the least complex and therefore the least costly. Poetry requiring varying and special indentions, line breaks, and spacing can be expensive and is usually not susceptible to the character count approach. Manuscripts involving scientific or technical terms, symbols, and formulae will usually be priced at the upper end of the pricing spectrum, as will texts or portions of texts in a foreign language.

It is impossible to price typesetting by the final printed page without knowing the size and average character width of the type to be used, the space (leading) to be allowed between lines, the line length, and the number of lines and columns per page. All of these factors have a direct bearing on the total number of characters on a given page and, depending on the combination, can vary this total character count by 300 percent.

A major cost factor is the condition of the manuscript itself. If a manuscript is amateurishly prepared, with frequent misspellings, inserts, strikeovers, duplications, omissions, punctuation that must be corrected, and illegible characters, an operator's productivity can be reduced by 50 percent, which means a 100 percent increase in cost.

You can usually anticipate that manual typesetting cost will range from $5 to $10 per page for simple 5½" x 8½" or 6" x 9" books. Larger page sizes usually involve proportionately higher character counts with equally higher costs.

Recent advances in computer and electronic technologies have had an enormous impact on typesetting methods and costs. Under certain conditions, manuscripts can now be optically scanned, received over telephone lines, or directly from computer disks—any one of which can reduce typesetting costs from 40 to 50 percent. Similar advances in electronic pagination and computer graphics now make it possible to eliminate the old 'cut-and-paste' methods of pagination, which can also reduce costs dramatically.

After type has been set, proofread, and corrected in galleys (long strips of unpaginated type), the third item of fixed cost—pagination—can be commenced. If offset printing is being used, galleys are waxed (rubber cement is sometimes used, but is less desirable), cut apart, positioned onto preprinted sheets, and burnished into place.

The main factors affecting pagination costs are the number of laydowns on each page and the judgmental requirements involved. A simple, single-column page involving straight text, equal numbers of lines per page, and a page number will usually require only two or three laydowns per page. When galleys must be cut apart for illustrations or separate formula, the number of laydowns can easily double or triple.

When running heads, captions, separate section heads, multiple columns, and footnotes are required, the number of laydowns increase accordingly. Additional cost may also be incurred for rubylith windows (for half-tones) and veloxes (for line illustrations). When many dissimilar elements must be included on a page and fitted into restricted space allotments, considerable trial and error, and experimentation, may be required. This demands thought, skill, and creative judgment—which, in turn, means extra time and money.

You can usually anticipate that paging costs for simple format books will range from $2 to $4 per page, which can be reduced significantly if electronic pagination methods can be utilized. But costs can also increase substantially when things start getting complicated.

Negatives make up the final item of one-time costs in offset printing.

After all pagination is completed, proofed, and corrected, the individual pages are positioned onto large templates in such a manner that, when printed, they will fold down to the proper final page sequence. (This process is called imposition.) There will be one template for each side of each large sheet to be printed. Depending on the size press being used, a single template may contain eight, sixteen, thirty-two, or more individual pages of the book.

These templates are then photographed by a very large camera. The exposed negatives are then developed, fixed, washed, and dried, usually by an automatic processor. They are then positioned on and attached to an opaque masking sheet, which is then cut away from all image areas. The non-image areas of the negatives are opaqued to eliminate pinholes or marks which might print, and a final blueline proof is made and folded down to represent the finished book.

A few book printers around the country, including our own company, have recently added a new direct-image platemaking technology which eliminates the time bottlenecks and high costs of negatives. Others have also added computerized halftone cameras which produce screened photographs in positive, rather than negative, form. Combining these new technologies, they are able to produced positive, camera-ready templates which are photographed directly by very large platemakers to produce press-ready plates. These plates are then mounted directly onto the presses, without negatives or masking, for printing. The savings involved, especially for short-run, high page count books with many photographs, can be very substantial, and the quality can be excellent.

Most professional book printers adhere rigidly to the policy that camera-ready copy must be of velox quality, with strong black and white images. This means that any light or faded illustrations, charts, etc. to be included from other sources (such as magazines or old books) must be strengthened with velox techniques at the pagination stage. Since all templates are exposed and developed at identical time-temperature-lens opening standards, any substandard original will tend to worsen when photographed—hence the policy.

When such procedures are followed, prices for negatives are largely a factor of the number of pages involved. The cost of a single-color line negative will usually range from $1 to $3 per book-size page, assuming 5½″ x 8½″ or 6″ x 9″ page sizes.

When multiple ink colors are to be used, however, an additional set of negatives will usually be required for each color, which will increase negative costs by at least an equal amount—and usually much more—for each color involved. If close registers, screens, or solids are required, the additional costs can be much higher.

Books that include continuous tone pictures will require separate halftone negatives which must be processed separately and stripped in individually onto the large base negatives. Halftone negatives will probably add from $6 to $12 for each picture included, depending on the quality and similarity of the originals, whether they can be gang shot or must be photographed individually, and the quality required. (If the computerized, positive-halftone camera, previously described, can be used these costs will, of course, be reduced considerably.)

All of the costs described above are one-time costs and should not recur unless changes are made in the book's content or design. They will remain constant whether the number of books to be printed is one, one thousand, or one million. With the possible exception of storage and filing costs, you should never have to pay for them again, whether your book goes into one or one hundred reprintings. They represent a fixed capital investment in your project which will, hopefully, be recouped many times over.

Continuing costs are very different. They are almost directly relatable to both the number of pages and the number of books to be produced, and they will recur each time your book is reprinted. They include: presswork, paper, and binding. (The cost of plates, in modern offset printing, is so low that most book printers feel it is less expensive to discard them after each printing than to preserve and store them, especially since a large percentage will usually be damaged in storage and have to be remade anyway.)

While on each printing there will be certain fixed, flat costs in each operation (job make-ready, plate make-ready, machine set up, and make-ready paper spoilage), these costs are relatively small and inconsequential when several thousand books are being produced.

The cost of presswork will depend largely on the book printer's equipment and area of specialization. Some printers use presses that print in increments of 5½" x 8½" and 8½" x 11" page sizes, (17½" x 23", 23" x 35", etc.). Others have presses that can print in increments of 6" x 9" (19" x 25", 25" x 38", etc.). Other increments are also used for special markets.

A printer who uses presses of the 5½" x 8½" group will be at a major cost disadvantage if he is asked to print a 6" x 9" book. In fact, his press cost can be almost twice as high since he must usually print the book as though it were an 8½" x 11" size, producing only half the number of pages with each press run. But a printer with a 6" x 9" capability has little problem—or cost penalty—at all with the smaller size since he merely reduces the sheet size to be printed.

Printers with small, single-color presses (19" x 25" and 25" x 38") will have low make-ready costs and will usually be competitive on book run quantities up to about 5,000 books. Printers with large perfecting presses, which usually require two operators and a much higher hourly charge, will have relatively higher make-ready costs, but will increasingly overcome them as the press runs becomes longer. Printers with large and very expensive, multi-operator web presses will have very high hourly cost rates and make-ready costs, but will be able to produce books at a lower unit cost when runs exceed 50,000 copies or so, due to the very high speed at which these presses can operate.

The cost of paper, within any single grade, finish, and color group, is almost directly proportionate to its weight. For example, 60 lb. paper costs about 20 percent more than 50 lb.; 70 lb. paper costs about 17 percent more than 60 lb.; and 80 lb. paper costs about 15 percent more than 70 lb. Since paper can easily constitute 20 to 30 percent of a book's total cost, such differences are obviously important and have a major influence on the list price which must be charged for the book.

Some book printers handle some or all of their binding requirements in-plant, but many find that they can give their clients competitive prices and faster turnaround by utilizing the services of the large, specialized bookbinders located in most major cities. This is especially true with hardback binding which, to be produced economically, involves extremely expensive, fully automated equipment, and a very high level of craftsmanship.

Whether handled in-plant or on a sub-contract basis, the costs are usually about the same. The main differences depend on the kind of binding used and the size equipment employed.

Saddle stitching is the least expensive binding method available, costing only a few cents per copy in larger quantities. Plastic element binding, usually used for smaller quantity books, may cost from $.75 to $1.50 per book, depending on the number of pages involved. Perfect binding will generally run from $.25 to $.50 per book in moderate page counts.

The cost of hardback binding is controlled largely by the equipment used by the bindery. Many large bookbinders still bind hardback books by hand, at costs of from $10 to $20 per book, in small quantities. Others have semi-automated equipment for medium-run jobs which can bring costs down to about $2 to $4 per book. Still other bookbinders pursue the very long run markets with extremely expensive, fully automated systems which can reduce costs to from $.75 to $1.50 per book, or less, depending largely on quantity, page count, and materials used.

Schedules and Deadlines

Planning and scheduling are central to a book printer's operation. Only with such controls is he able to produce the number of books that his substantial investment demands, with a minimum number of emergencies and bottlenecks, and to provide his clients with the maximum value for each dollar spent. Modern book printing is a highly specialized, thoroughly organized, work-flow system which relies on deadlines being met and promises being kept by everyone, at every stage of the process.

Successful book printers are busy book printers. Even in relatively small plants they will produce hundreds of titles every year. At any single point in time they may have a dozen or more books in process at each production center: typesetting, paging, camera, pressroom, and bindery. The only way they can function effectively is to schedule jobs in advance, and the further the better. Any book printer with modern facilities could turn out any single title in a very short length of time, often within a week or so. But to handle hundreds of books requires careful planning and advance scheduling.

The reliability of the book printer's clients is crucial to the success of such a system. Manuscripts must be delivered when they are promised. Partial or late deliveries create major problems. Most book printers do not—and cannot—approach the production of a book on a 'piecemeal' basis. With the high-speed (and high-cost) equipment now being used, they are forced to produce each job as a single, total package.

Manuscripts should be delivered complete in every detail. This includes not only the manuscript itself but all art work, pictures, drawings, tables, the ISBN number, the Library of Congress number, copyright information, cover, spine, and dust jacket copy, front material, back material, and any permissions that may be required. Delays may cause the book to require rescheduling, often by several weeks.

It is always a good idea to develop a checklist, well in advance, covering all of the elements which must be furnished to the book printer by the deadline agreed on. Such a list should have columns listing the elements involved, the date each was submitted, the items still due, and the date they are expected. If the book is an involved, multi-author book, originating from many distant locations, this check list should be expanded to include individual papers or chapters, dates proofs are received and returned, etc.

When special typographic characters will be required, the book printer should be furnished with a list of such characters, at least sixty days in advance. If a special style sheet is required, it should also be furnished.

* * *

When the author finally completes his exhausting work on his manuscript he wants to see it in print—fast. Preferably the next day!

But the production of your book is a complex, multi-faceted process involving many separate production steps which must be completed in sequence. Shortcuts and emergency scheduling almost invariably result in errors, poor quality, 'redos,' unhappy clients, frustrated employees, irritation, and usually end up taking more time than if normal procedures and precautions had been followed in the first place.

Here are the steps usually involved in the production of your book:

1. Production conference with client.
2. Manuscript submitted and analyzed.
3. Manuscript is marked for typesetters.
4. Type is set in galley form.
5. Galleys proofed in-house.
6. Xerox copies sent to client.
7. Client proofreads galleys.
8. Galley proofs returned with corrections.
9. Corrections made to galleys.
10. Galleys reviewed by editor.
11. Galleys released for paging.
12. Preliminary paging completed.
13. Cover type set.
14. Running heads and page numbers set.
15. Table of Contents and index set and proofed.
16. Final paging completed.
17. Page proofs prepared and sent to client.
18. Page proofs returned with corrections.
19. Page proof corrections set and applied.
20. Imposition dummy prepared.

21. Job reviewed and checked by editor.
22. Job released for camera.
23. Camera layup made on templates.
24. Line negatives shot.
25. Halftone negatives shot.
26. Negatives stripped and opaqued.
27. Blueline proofs prepared and sent to client.
28. Blueline proofs returned.
29. Corrections (if any) made.
30. Printing plates made.
31. Presswork completed on inside sheets.
32. Presswork completed on cover or dust jacket.
33. Sheets folded to pre-trim size.
34. Signatures gathered and bound.
35. Books are trimmed.
36. Entire job is inspected.
37. Packaging and cartoning completed.
38. Job is shipped to client.

All of the preceding steps, and more if the book is to be hardbound, must be carefully completed on most books being manufactured. Each step must be completed with care and in the proper sequence. Some will only take a short time, but others may require one or more full production days depending on the size of the job. Each job must be carefully coordinated with dozens of similar jobs for other clients that are going through the plant at the same time.

For all of these reasons, the author/publisher should control his delivery requirement, in advance, to allow the full measure of time needed to produce the job in an accurate, attractive, and professional manner.

Terms, Conditions and Industry Customs

Quotation Acceptance. Most book printers furnish their quotations in duplicate. If you accept the conditions and price of the quotation, you will be asked to sign one copy and return it to their office as soon as possible so that production space can be reserved for your book. Since most book printers schedule production over three to six month periods, this can be important in being sure that your delivery requirements are met.

Price Changes. Most quoted prices are guaranteed firm for 30 days from date of quotation. Quotations not accepted within 30 days are subject to review and change to reflect cost and pricing variations which may have occurred.

Terms of Payment. Credit arrangements, if required, should be made with the book printer's credit department at the time the quotation is accepted. If not, payment in full may be required in advance. Some book printers offer payment terms similar to the following: 1/3 with order, 1/3 at blueline proof, and 1/3 upon delivery.

Progress Billings. Jobs involving more than 60 days of production time will usually be progress-billed monthly on the basis of work completed and material used and/or held in stock for a particular job.

Ownership. The Printing Industry Standards state that all supplemental materials furnished by a printer for use in the production of a printing job remain the property of the printer. This includes original typeset galleys, negatives, halftones, veloxes, and plates. If other arrangements are desired they should be negotiated in advance.

Overs and Unders. Unless stated otherwise in the quotation, quantities will be furnished subject to a ±10 percent variance allowance which will be charged or credited at the per 1000 price quoted after allowance for one-time flat charges (i.e., typesetting, negatives, halftones, veloxes, plates, etc.). Orders produced within this variance may, at the printer's option, be considered as complete. If exact quantities are required, arrangements should be negotiated in advance.

The Small-Press Movement

Authors with talents and interests which extend beyond writing into areas of graphics and mechanics have, for centuries, involved themselves in the actual production of their books. This usually meant the purchase of a small, hand-operated letterpress and a selection of hand-set type, all of which could fit into the kitchen, basement, or attic. A few have even had the courage to attempt the bindery operations required.

Beginning in the early 1960's these isolated and independent efforts, which were avocational, began to take on a recognizable form which can now be identified as the small-press movement. A fascinating and informative history of this movement is presented in *The Publish-It Yourself Handbook*, edited by Bill Henderson and published by The Pushcart Book Press. The real-life stories of 27 small-press publishers are outlined in as many chapters. Each offers its own agony and its own ecstacy; each contains its own lessons from its own perspective. It is a marvelous, extremely useful book which should be in every self-publisher's personal library.

In retrospect, a movement of this kind was probably inevitable.

The trade publishing industry was emerging from a severe recession with major economic problems, and was facing the necessity of a reorientation to more economically viable policies. The result was that more and more doors were closed to new, unknown, and non-commercial authors.

Simultaneously, the involvement and emotional outpourings of the period demanded avenues of expression. The possibilities were largely denied, partly for commercial reasons and partly for philosophical and political reasons. As the 60s ended, an era of highly charged personal actions and reactions also ended, leaving a creative reservoir which required form and expression. The small-press movement offered the release such pent-up pressures demanded. Of the possibilities available, few are more fulfilling than writing, producing, and publishing one's own books.

While writing is an important extension of self it can also involve great frustration. A writer, like an actor or a painter, needs an audience. He needs the feedback which an audience provides for his efforts. He needs the applause and the acclaim, even the rebuke and the bad reviews. At least he exists. Being published, in whatever manner, provides such feedback.

Many, perhaps most, of those writers involved in the small-press movement are non-commercial, often by choice, usually as a result of the extreme independence of their natures. They insist on saying what they want to say, the way they want to say it, without regard for commercial consequences. They want to control not only their words and their art, but the way in which they are put on paper, printed, and bound. They do not want to relinquish that control to anyone—not to editors, not to printers, not to other publishers. To achieve this objective, they are willing to accept the potential consequences of both severely limited markets and possible losses.

A few are so talented, and the quality of their product so extraordinary, that they are able to resist compromise and still find eventual commercial acceptance. Some achieve remarkable sales and profit, usually through later take-overs by established trade publishers. Others are content to remain small—the smaller the better—and to find their personal fulfillment in what, to them, is a total art form.

* * *

It is far beyond the scope of this book to present the how-to-do-it techniques of book production in this environment. It should be noted, however, that innovations of the past 20 years within the printing industry now offer new and remarkable opportunities for the dedicated author-craftsman. Such innovations now make quality book production, in small quantities, available to all with the courage, talent, and energy to accept the challenges involved.

Chapter 3

The Manuscript

There is a broad consensus within the book industry concerning proper and acceptable methods of manuscript preparation. The procedures involved are equally valid whether you are submitting your work to a trade publisher or, as a self-publisher, to a book printer. While some of the rules are based on tradition, most are soundly grounded on a long history of trial and error. In all cases the objective is the same: to communicate the author's message and intentions in a clear, organized, and accurate manner that leaves no room for question, doubt, or misinterpretation.

This is a far bigger order than it may seem. The opportunities for error and misunderstandings are almost endless. And every wrong decision can create a sequence of corrections which are not only costly but may well diminish the quality of the final book.

How Manuscripts Are Processed

When a manuscript is submitted to a trade publisher, the first step is its evaluation for publication. If accepted, however, this is only the beginning. It will be carefully copy edited for consistency of style, spelling, punctuation, grammar, completeness, organization, and factual accuracy. A copy will be forwarded to the design department for the development of an overall design, which will include the selection of type styles, paging formats, cover design and dust jacket design. The manuscript will then be marked for the typesetter to indicate type styles, sizes, faces, line lengths, leading between lines, indentions, and dozens of other production instructions. Much of this information will be written on the manuscript itself.

When the manuscript is received by the typesetter/printer—from whatever source—he will compute and quote a firm, lump sum price for the book's production. This requires an accurate character count of the manuscript, both to estimate typesetting charges and to determine the total page count of the book, from which other production estimates will be made.

The much-marked manuscript is then assigned to one or more typesetters who work on an hourly basis and are expected to produce (typeset) a predetermined number of characters per day based on the kind of work to be done. They have usually never seen the manuscript before, never met the author, and may know little about the subject covered.

Most professional typesetters purposely avoid 'reading' as they set type—they see only individual characters, and those at a very high rate of speed. Speed and accuracy are essential if the typesetter is to be competitive. Minutes count. A rhythm is established and speed increases. But one illegible character, the questionable spelling of a single word, or any omitted instruction can bring it all to a halt—and cost the equivalent of 10,000 characters per hour not set.

Finally that same manuscript becomes the authoritative basis for proofing galleys, first by the typesetter's proofreaders, often by the editor, and finally by the author. And it becomes the arbiter in deciding which corrections are chargeable to the printer and which are chargeable to the author.

The manuscript is, therefore, a very important and valuable document for all concerned. As such, it demands and deserves a high degree of professional skill in its preparation.

Parts of a Book

A professionally prepared manuscript must contain certain basic elements before being submitted to a publisher or printer. If parts are missing, a notification should be included that they are 'to come' and when they can be expected. While not all manuscripts will include all of the elements listed, the following will serve as a check list:

Front Material
Title Page
Dedication
Epigraph
Table of Contents
List of Illustrations
List of Tables
Foreword
Preface
Acknowledgements
Introduction

Body Material
All text matter
Footnotes
Tables

Back Material
Appendix
Notes
Glossary
Bibliography
Index

Additional Material
Illustrations
Captions
Maps and Charts

If your book is being self-published and the manuscript is going directly to the book printer, it should also include, where applicable, the half-title page, copyright information, ISBN number, Library of Congress number, a list of running heads, all finished artwork to be furnished, and information for the cover, spine, and dust jacket.

Half Title. Sometimes called the 'bastard' title, this is usually the very first right-hand (recto) page of the book after the end sheet, preceded only by the *Frontispiece*, when used. It should only include the book's main title, usually in smaller print, and should not include the subtitle, author's name, or publisher's name.

Title Page. The next right-hand page is the title page. It includes the main title, the subtitle, edition number, name of the author, editor or translator, the name and location of the publisher, and the publisher's logo (colophon). The title page may be a two-page spread, if desired, or the preceding blank page may be used for other information, such as a list of the author's previous publications.

Copyright Page. Under the new copyright law, which became effective January 1, 1978, the copyright notice may be located in any position that will give reasonable notice of the claim of copyright. However, the traditional location on the left-hand (verso) page following the title page is still the most practical, and is recommended. The word copyright is usually, but not necessarily, spelled out, followed by the copyright symbol ©, the year of copyright, and the name of the copyright holder. Additional information may include subsequent editions copyrighted and the date of each, the statement 'All Rights Reserved,' the publishing history of the book, the publisher's address, the International Standard Book Number (ISBN), the Library of Congress number, and the name of the country in which the book was printed.

Dedication. The dedication page may be as general or specific as the author desires, and is usually titled simply 'To' or 'For.' Extravagant or humorous dedications are rarely used today. The dedication should be placed on a right-hand page.

Epigraph. An epigraph is usually a short poem or a quotation that sets the overall theme, tone, or philosophy of the book. It is followed by its author's name (last name only if renowned) and, sometimes, the title of the book from which it is taken. The epigraph may be placed on either a right-hand or a left-hand page.

Table of Contents. If the table of contents requires only one page it should be positioned for a right-hand page; if two pages, it is often easier for the reader if it starts on a left-hand page. The table of contents should at least include the title and page numbers of all parts and chapters, and any elements that are included in the back material. As a book becomes more technical or scientific in nature the table of contents will become progressively more detailed. Reference-oriented books should include a very comprehensive listing to provide readers quick access to the information they need to locate.

Since the author doesn't know the final page numbers when the original table of contents is being prepared he can either omit page numbers completely, record them as '000' to indicate that they must be added later, or insert the page numbers of the manuscript itself. If the latter course is followed the numbers should be circled to remind the typesetter to change them during typesetting.

List of Illustrations. When a book contains many illustrations, especially when they are full-page illustrations or will be referred to frequently, a list of illustrations may be desirable. If the illustrations are to be printed separately by letterpress, as opposed to offset printing, and consequently without page numbers, the terms 'following page' and 'facing page' are often used to provide location reference. Such illustrations are usually called plates and numbered sequentially throughout the book. Illustrations printed by the offset method—as is usually the case—and, consequently, incorporated into the normal page number sequence will simply be listed by title and page number. Illustrations are usually listed on a right-hand page.

List of Tables. When many important and full-page tables are included, a list of tables may be desirable, usually listed on a right-hand page.

Foreword. A foreword (not forward) is a statement by someone other than the author, usually about either the book or the author. It can be as long or as short as necessary, is followed by the name of its author, and should be located on a right-hand page.

Preface/Acknowledgments. This page is usually used by the author to discuss any special reasons for writing the book, special methodology that requires explanation, and acknowledgments to those who provided him with information or assistance. It should generally be kept as short as possible with more lengthy discussions being made, when necessary, in the introduction. The preface should always be placed on a right-hand page. Acknowledgments may be incorporated into the preface or, when lengthy, placed on a separate page by themselves.

Introduction. An introduction that is not directly related to the text itself should be included with the front material. If, however, it is really a prelude to and part of the text, setting the scene or the tone for that which follows, it should be a part of the text material. Introductions should always start on a right-hand page.

Parts or Sections. Some books lend themselves to separation into two or more major parts or sections. This may be done by chronological separation, geographic separation, major changes in the direction of the story, or for other reasons. Parts may be identified by number, title, or both. Each new part should start on a right-hand page followed by a left-hand blank page preceding the text which follows.

Chapters. Most books are divided into chapters which are numbered consecutively throughout the book, even when part separations are used. Chapters may be numbered, titled, or both, and should be as nearly similar in length as the text allows. Titles, when used, should be as short and indicative as possible, especially in serious, nonfiction books. Clever, ambiguous titles make it unnecessarily difficult for the prospective buyer/reader to evaluate the book, and for research-oriented readers to quickly locate specific areas of interest. Long titles create problems with running heads and are usually avoidable.

Each new chapter should, by first preference, begin on a right-hand page, especially if reprints of individual chapters are contemplated, or if the book is short (under 160 pages or so). It is entirely acceptable, however, for chapters to begin on left-hand pages, especially in very long books where page count becomes critical. Certain types of books, especially those involving many very short chapters or sections, may use *run-in chapters,* where one chapter ends and a new one begins on the same page. When this method must be used an adequate amount of vertical separation should be allowed between chapters.

In the original manuscript itself, new chapters should start at least three inches down from the common top margin. Chapter titles should be centered and typed with initial caps only, followed by four vertical typewriter spaces. The first line of the first paragraph following may, if desired, be set flush left without indention, even though indention may be used on all remaining paragraphs. Alternatively, the first line may be set with standard indention or double-standard indention. (It may also, when typeset, be set in all small caps with the first letter being a *stickup* or *drop display initial,* but this is not normally indicated by the manuscript typist.)

In multi-author books the author's name may appear under the chapter title with his affiliation shown in a footnote.

Subheads. The various levels of subheads must follow the organizational structure of the table of contents and be clearly differentiated by consistent placement. Here is one placement plan that is frequently used and is workable:

A-level subheads are centered on the page. *B-level subheads* start at the left margin (flush left) and on a separate line from the following text. *C-level subheads* are usually printed in italics, begin a paragraph, and are followed by a period. This lowest-level subhead is sometimes called a *run-in side head.*

Subhead titles should be kept as short and as indicative as possible, and should follow a similar tone or style throughout the manuscript. Capitalize first letters only, except prepositions, articles, and coordinate conjunctions. Do not end A- or B-level subheads with periods. Do not include C-level subheads as an extension of the text; repeat the information within the text if necessary. It is not necessary that all subhead levels be used in every chapter if they are not needed. Any one or all may be either used or omitted.

Extracts. Extracts and long quotations are usually indented from the left margin a space equal to the standard indent being used, but usually not less than five typewriter spaces, to set them apart. Extra space should be left above and below. Extracts from poetry should follow the original design for indention and be centered on the page.

Footnotes. Footnotes should be typed, double-spaced, and separated by chapter numbers or titles. Start each footnote on a separate line, indented, and ending with a period. Footnotes should be numbered consecutively within each chapter, with the number followed by a period and a space. Corresponding numbers within the text must follow the footnoted information and be typed above the line.

It should be remembered that footnotes are just that— notes at the foot. They should be as brief and take up as little space as their objectives will allow.

Tables. Tables should be typed, single-spaced, on separate sheets from text material. Table number identification must be typed above each table. Approximate locations of tables, desired by the author, should be indicated by referencing circled table numbers in the margin of the manuscript. All columns must be precisely aligned. Column heads and other data must be accurately positioned so that there can be no question as to what goes with what.

Appendix. Though not necessary for many books, an appendix can be very useful to serious readers of nonfiction books. It allows room for the inclusion of lengthy, often technical, supporting material which is not necessary for all readers and would unduly complicate the text.

Appendices are always included in the back material, usually preceding the glossary, bibliography, and index. They should be designated by number (Appendix 1, Appendix 2, etc.) or by letter (Appendix A, Appendix B, etc.) and titled. They are usually, though not necessarily, set in smaller type size, like excerpts in the text. Unlike excerpts, which are indented, they are set to the same line length as the text itself.

The first appendix should start on a right-hand page, but additional appendices may start on either right- or left-hand pages as they fall.

If a section for 'Notes' is included, it should follow the appendix.

Glossary. If a glossary is included it should be typed on separate sheets with each word to be defined, typed flush left in alphabetical order without a period. Leave about five spaces after the longest word to establish a common left margin for all definitions. Multi-line definitions should align with that common margin. If all definitions include one sentence or less, no period should be used; otherwise, periods should be used for ending all sentences. A similar procedure should be used when a list of abbreviations is included.

Bibliography. The bibliography should be typed in alphabetical order by author, double-spaced, on separate sheets, with additional spacing allowed between each listing. Authors' names are listed last name first, flush left on the sheet. Additional lines of multi-line listings should be indented about five spaces. When several works by the same author are included type three hyphens, instead of his name, for each additional listing. If a period was used after the author's name in the initial listing, a period should also follow the hyphens.

Each book listing should include, in order, all of the following that are applicable: name of author(s), editor(s), or sponsoring institution; full title and subtitle of book; series; volume number; edition; city of publication; publisher's name; year of publication. The title of the book will be typeset in italics. After the period following the author's name, commas separate all additional entries, except that a period precedes and a colon follows the city of publication.

Listings of articles from periodicals should include: name of author; title of article; name of periodical; volume number or date; page reference.

Clarity, completeness, and consistency are the goal of acceptable bibliographies. Abbreviations may be used and reasonable changes of style are acceptable, but whatever form is finally adopted, it must be adhered to consistently throughout.

Index. The importance of a comprehensive cross-index in any non-fiction book intended for continuing use and reference by the reader cannot be overestimated. No reader has the time to endlessly search for the data he needs, and the utility of any publication is vastly diminished when he is required to do so. The value of thousands of otherwise excellent books is seriously diluted due to the lack of care and thought given to their indexing.

The manual activities of index preparation are the responsibility of the author and are not usually included in prices quoted by the book printer unless specifically stated to the contrary.

There is simply no shortcut to *manual indexing*. It is, at best, a slow, time-consuming activity. But it can be approached methodically and without the confusion and frustration that often accompanies the task.

There is only one workable approach—start at the beginning and proceed to the end, page by page, item by item, writing each piece of data onto individual index cards or slips of paper, in as many cross-referencing forms as the reader might realistically think of, with the page number for each. When the entire book has been covered in this manner, the cards can then be alphabetized, consolidated under similar titles and names where appropriate, and then typed in the desired form, indicating indents, emphasis, etc.

Letter-by-letter alphabetizing is recommended. The index should be typed flush left, double-spaced, and limited to a single column for each sheet.

Indexing cannot be done until the book has been typeset and paginated with page numbers applied.

With the advent of personal computers, indexing software has also become available. A hard disk is almost always required. Computer indexing operates on a 'flagging' system. Words that are to be indexed must be flagged within the text itself, either as it is developed or added later. Once flagged in this manner, all such words can be sorted as desired and may then be printed out in hardcopy form for the typesetter. If your typesetter has the capability of interfacing with your computer, the index can then be set in type without additional keystroking.

Relational data base software, such as dBASE III, may also be used for indexing. However, the words to be indexed will usually have to be typed. The advantage of this approach is that sorting is simple and fast, and the resulting files can be used by the typesetter without rekeying.

Illustrations. Pictures, photographs, drawings, and other artwork should be protected by heavy cardboard and put in a separate, clearly identified envelope when mailed. If the items are too large for an envelope, a mailing tube may be used. Illustration reference numbers should be written out of the image area in the margin or with a soft marker on the back of photographs. Crop marks for photographs can be made with a grease pencil or marker by short horizontal and vertical lines in the white border, or on the back if there is no border.

Corresponding illustration numbers should be included on the accompanying list of captions and noted in the margin of the manuscript itself, circled at the approximate location desired.

Captions. Some authorities define a caption as the title of an illustration and refer to the explanations or descriptions of those illustrations as legends. Others within the industry use the word caption to cover both.

A listing of captions (including headings and descriptions) should accompany the illustrations in the envelope or mailing tube containing them. Illustrations are usually designated as *figures* and are numbered consecutively throughout the book (Fig. 1, Fig. 2, etc.). If photographs are to be printed separately by letterpress they will be given their own numbering sequence.

Running Heads. A running head is a page caption that 'runs' across the top of most pages of a book. While not all books require running heads, and they increase cost somewhat, they enhance a book's appearance, utility, and stature in the eyes of most readers.

Manuscripts being submitted to trade publishers need not include a listing of running heads since they will be developed by the publisher's editor. Self-publishers, however, should develop such a list for the book printer and it should accompany the original manuscript.

Title designations and locations for running heads are subject to a great deal of variance. Probably the most popular style is to place the book's title on left-hand pages and the various chapter titles on right-hand pages. If the book is divided into parts the part title can be used on left-hand pages and chapter titles on right-hand pages. Books with chapters or sections by different authors may have the book or chapter title on the left with the author(s) name on the right.

Running head titles may be centered, placed flush with the page margin, or placed next to the page number itself separated by a dash or diagonal. Running heads are not usually used in front material, on blank pages, or on pages with only illustrations or tables, unless there are many such pages in sequence.

Since only a limited amount of space is available across the top of the pages, titles should be kept as short as possible. Type sizes smaller than that used for the text itself are often used, with face selection (italic, bold, etc.) being a matter of individual preference.

Typing the Manuscript

Manuscripts should be typed on white, 8½" x 11" paper. The paper should be of reasonably heavy weight and a good grade. A No. 1 grade of 20 lb. bond is very acceptable; a No. 4 grade can be used if corrections will not be made by eraser. Never use 'erasable' papers; they smear when handled and are slippery. They also create problems if the manuscript is to be optically scanned.

An electric typewriter equipped with lift-off correcting ribbon is ideal. Standard electrics are also usually satisfactory if corrections are made carefully. If a manual typewriter is used, be sure that the keys are adjusted and cleaned, and use a fresh, black ribbon. Do not use red/black combinations or colored ribbons.

Carbon copies can be made if desired. However, the most efficient technique is to prepare a single, perfect original manuscript and then to duplicate the additional copies required. You should *always* keep at least one corrected copy in your permanent files; most publishers will eventually require two copies. If simultaneous submissions will be made to several publishers, copies will be needed for the number of publishers anticipated. It is essential that the photocopier being used have an ample supply of toner and be in perfect working order. Fuzzy characters, wavy lines, streaks, splotches, etc., are not acceptable to trade publishers.

Type on only one side of the paper. Leave a minimum one inch margin all around. Each line should be typed to a reasonably consistent average line length; each full page should include approximately the same number of lines. Either pica or elite type is acceptable, but one or the other must be used throughout the manuscript.

Double-space between all lines of text; never single-space except for tables. When extra spacing is desired, leave three spaces.

Never type over characters to make corrections. Either delete the old characters with white correcting opaque, or erase them. When necessary, a word may be ruled out (using hyphens or a black-ink pen) and the correct word added in the space directly above. It is not necessary that a manuscript be void of final corrections. It *is* necessary that such corrections be made in a neat, legible hand, in black ink, and in a completely clear manner. Words, sentences, or paragraphs may be deleted by simply drawing a single horizontal line through all words to be deleted.

Do not make corrections in the margin or draw arrows to indicate changes of position. Do not ask that copy be picked up and inserted from other sections. Do not paste slips of paper on the bottom of manuscript pages which must be folded up. If major changes or transitions are required, cut the page apart, type and insert the change in the proper place, and tape the pieces to a new sheet in the proper sequence. Or, retype the entire page.

When frequent diacritical marks and symbols are included, a typewriter equipped with such keys should be used, if possible. If not, they can be inserted, carefully and clearly, by hand, using a fine point pen with black ink.

Every page of an original manuscript must be numbered, preferably in the upper right corner. Numbering may be done with a hand numbering machine, using a freshly inked pad, by hand, or by typewriter. Pages added after the manuscript has been numbered must be identified by using the preceding page number plus an alphabetic suffix (122A, 122B, etc.). To avoid error the page preceding and following such additions should reference the addition. For example, '122A follows' and 'follows 122B.'

Pages of front material included in the manuscript will eventually be numbered with lower case Roman numerals. If the manuscript is being prepared by a self-publisher to be sent directly to a book printer, every page of front material which will appear in the final book should be enclosed, including blank pages marked 'blank.'

Page numbers in the final typeset book may follow any one of several format possibilities. They may be centered at the bottom margin, or positioned to the outside margin at either the bottom or top of the page. If running heads are used, page numbers will usually be positioned to the left (on left-hand pages) or right outside margin (on right-hand pages) on line with the running head at the top of the page.

The book industry has standardized on a page numbering system which requires odd numbers to be used on right-hand pages and even numbers to be used on lefthand pages. All production systems are designed for, and all craftsmen are trained for, this system. *It must be followed.*

Page numbers are not used on the first pages of new chapters or new parts. They are also omitted on display pages of the front material, such as the half-title page, title page, copyright page, dedication, foreword, epigraph, etc. Page numbers are not usually used on pages containing only tables or illustrations, unless they are presented in a multi-page sequence.

Computers and Word Processors. If you own a personal computer, a printer, and a good word processing software package, you already know how lucky you are. If you don't, and you plan on doing much writing in the future, I strongly urge that you purchase such a system. It may prove to be one of the best investments you have ever made. They can now be purchased at reasonable prices, with relatively small monthly payments.

Most of the suggestions given for *Typing the Manuscript* also apply to manuscripts prepared on computers or word processors. The good part is that, with computers, the final results are so much easier to achieve. If using a computer, your final manuscript should be perfect. There is no reason for final manual corrections or for the tedious cut-and-paste routine of rearranging paragraphs and sections.

A word of caution, however: If you do not have a laser printer and must print out your manuscript with a dot matrix printer, be sure it is operating properly and that you use a fresh ribbon.

Copyrighting Your Book

The latest copyright law—Public Law 94-553 (90 Stat. 2541)—became effective January 1, 1978. Copies are available at no charge from the Copyright Office, Library of Congress, Washington, D.C. 20559. For a complete summary of the new law, send $1.00 to Frieda Johnson, *Publisher's Weekly*, 249 W. 17th St, New York, N.Y. 10011.

The information that follows is limited to the copyrighting of books and book manuscripts, and mainly applies to copyrights obtained after January 1, 1978.

Duration of Copyright. The new law generally provides protection throughout the author's life plus an additional 50 years after the author's death.

For joint works, protection is based on the life and death of the last surviving author.

Unpublished works—in existence, not copyrighted, and not in the public domain on January 1, 1978—may be copyrighted with full protection.

Books written for hire, and anonymous and pseudonymous works (unless author's name is revealed in Copyright Office records), are protected for 100 years from creation or 75 years from publication, whichever is shorter.

Books copyrighted before January 1, 1978, and in their first 28 year term (under the old law), may have copyright protection renewed at the end of that term for an additional 47 years. If copyrighted books were in their second term of copyright on that date, they have been automatically extended for this new term and do not have to be renewed.

Notice of Copyright. The required form of copyright notice has not changed: the word 'Copyright' and/or the symbol ©; year of first publication; and the name of the owner of the copyright are required.

Under the new law the notice may be in any position that will give reasonable notice of the claim of copyright. For practical reasons, however, the back of the title page is still most desirable and is recommended.

'Publication' is defined as the distribution of copies of a work by sale (or other transfer) to the public. Offering to distribute copies constitutes publication.

Registration. The registration of a copyright claim may be made at any time during the copyright term. For non-dramatic literary works (books), request *Form TX* from the Information and Publication Section, Copyright Office, Library of Congress, Washington, D.C. 20559. Either published or unpublished works may be registered.

Send two copies of the printed book (one copy if in unpublished form), the properly executed application form, and a check for $10.00 made payable to the Register of Copyrights—all in one package—to: Register of Copyrights, Library of Congress, Washington, D.C. 20559.

While present interpretations state that registration can be completed at any time during the copyright term, it is recommended that this action be taken immediately after your books are printed. If your application is completed fully and accurately, and no questions are raised by the Copyright Office, you should receive your copy of the copyright registration form, with the registration number and official seal, in six weeks or less.

Use of an Attorney. Either you or a duly authorized agent can apply for your copyright. An experienced copyright attorney will probably charge from $50 to $75 to obtain your copyright; you can obtain your own for $10 plus time and postage.

The route you should take depends largely on what you believe to be the potential of your book. If you have any reason to feel that it may have really significant potential—economic or otherwise—you would be wise to use an attorney. While the procedure for doing-it-yourself is simple, mistakes can be made, and fortunes can be lost. It has happened.

ISBN Number

The International Standard Book Number (ISBN) is an integral part of a computerized system of book identification adopted by the U.S. book industry in 1968. It is now being used by most U.S. publishers.

The full ISBN number is actually made up of two numbers. A prefix number is assigned to each participating publisher which is repeated in each book he publishes. The variable numbers, which follow, identify individual titles and bindings released by that publisher. When a title is released in both hardback and paperback each is assigned a different number.

Each participating publisher is assigned an individual number and a log book which lists preassigned title numbers. As new titles are published they are written in the log by the publisher, the identifying number is printed in the book, and the agency is notified on the forms that are provided.

With the advent of CD-ROM storage system, the ISBN program is becoming even more important to all publishers. R. R. Bowker Company now publishes all *Books in Print* on compact disks for use in this system. Increasing numbers of books are now being searched for, located, and ordered electronically using this system, both nationally and internationally. Having your books clearly and completed listed in this system can significantly increase your sales and profits.

To participate in the program write to International Standard Book Numbering Agency, 245 W. 17th St., New York, N.Y. 10011.

Library of Congress Number

The Library of Congress makes its printed catalog cards available to libraries throughout the world. Since 1951 card numbers have been preassigned to certain forthcoming books. These numbers appear in book lists and reviews by the leading book trade journals and in many reference books.

Numbers are not assigned to books already in print; they must be assigned prior to publication. Requests should be sent to: Library of Congress, Cataloging in Publication Division, Washington, D.C. 20540. The following information is required: name of author (or editor); title of book; edition; date of publication; name and address of publisher; series information; copyright status; number of pages (approximately); and kind of binding.

Card numbers are not assigned to all publications, only to those which the Library intends to collect. The following are usually excluded: vanity press publications, booklets, manuals, elementary and secondary textbooks, light fiction, and others.

When a book is to be cataloged, a number is preassigned and forwarded to the publisher on a three-by-five-inch slip which shows the catalog card number, author, title, publisher, and publication date.

The preassigned number should be printed on the back of the title page, along with the copyright notice and ISBN number.

As soon as your book has been printed, and before the official publication date, you should send a complimentary copy to the CIP Office (address above). Postage-free labels are provided.

There is no charge for this service and it can often result in significant orders from totally unexpected sources and geographic locations. It is highly recommended.

Editing

The editor is usually the 'man (or woman) in charge' of all books to which he or she is assigned—from beginning to end. He has one basic responsibility: to make certain that a truly first-rate, professional product is released to the market.

In many ways, and especially with some authors, the editor makes the most vital of all contributions to a book's success, for the finest craftsmanship in production and the most expensive marketing will not keep a second-rate product sold.

While the editor's first responsibility will necessarily be to those who employ him, he also works for the author—or at least in partnership with him—to be absolutely certain that *nothing* is left to chance which might in any way detract from the possibilities of a book reaching its full potential.

Editors vary in skill, experience, and character like everyone else. But at their best they are leaders and motivators who can bring out the very best that an author has in him—an author's friend, advisor, and mentor.

Editing responsibilities vary depending on the method of publishing. When a book is being handled by a trade publisher, final responsibility rests with the publisher's editor assigned to the book, although the author is expected to complete as much self-editing as his training and experience make possible. The author is also expected to read, understand, and abide by the publisher's announced 'guides to style.' (Style, in this sense, means 'the rules of uniformity in matters of punctuation, capitalization, word division, spelling, and other details of expression—many of which may vary according to custom.'—*A Manual of Style*)

When a book is being self-published, the final responsibility shifts to the author/publisher. While he may delegate it to free-lance editors, editors employed by the book specialist, or even to the book printer, the burden of final responsibility cannot be avoided.

Kinds of Editing. There are three distinctly different kinds of editing: *editing for content, editing for style* (as defined above), and *editing for production.*

Editing for content, the most creative and time-consuming form of editing, involves the editor in an in-depth evaluation and understanding of the book from the perspective of the reader. Does the book have basic reader appeal? Will it attract and hold the reader's interest? Are all explanations and descriptions clear and comprehensible? Is the logic and organization of the presentation sound? Does it flow smoothly and flawlessly toward the desired objectives? If the book is a work of fiction, are the characterizations strong, does the plot unfold smoothly? Do the elements of conflict, suspense, and climax all fit into the overall structure at appropriate points? Are some sections too wordy and others treated too lightly? Is there so much description that it kills interest; is there enough to clarify the parameters for the reader? These and dozens of other considerations are a part of the creative editing process.

Writers love to write, and they love words (especially their own). If they didn't they would surely be in a different profession. But this obsession with words can frequently become a problem. However diligently a writer may attempt to organize his manuscript and to structure his logic, once he takes pen-in-hand and words begin to flow, it is almost inevitable that, from time to time, he will ignore or forget his carefully constructed outline and begin to write for the simple joy of writing. When this happens the logic of the presentation may be weakened and gaping holes may appear in the organization of the material. The problem, as in proofreading one's own copy, is that writers tend to 'read in' such voids in their own minds, quite literally not seeing them. Or, as sometimes happens, they may simply be incapable of destroying their own beloved words with a blue pencil.

An editor, however, is not entangled in this same emotional web. From his detached position he is able to view the author's work with far greater objectivity, to read and think in logical and organized frameworks, and to more accurately place himself at the vantage point of the ultimate reader. Once this is accomplished, any wooden, wordy, confused portions of a manuscript can be transformed, to take their appropriate place within the whole.

The editor cannot—and must not—change the writer's personal writing style, and he cannot do the writer's job for him. But he *can* become a friendly and supportive devil's advocate, suggesting areas that could benefit from rewrites, additions, or deletions.

Of all forms of editing, this is the most valuable—and the most difficult to find. First, because it requires a level of creativity, judgment, and caring that is rare in any profession. Second, because, when properly done, it can be very time consuming and expensive, regardless of who may be paying the bill.

Editing for style requires, first of all, a solid technical foundation in the language itself, such as that which should be obtained (but often isn't) in four years of college English. Beyond this, however, it requires a complete familiarity with the practices and traditions of the book publishing industry and an intimate knowledge of the various manuals of style that are acceptable to that industry. Many such manuals are available. One of the most popular and comprehensive is *A Manual of Style*, published by The University of Chicago Press. If an author/publisher could have but one style manual in his personal library, it might well be this one.

It is far beyond the scope of this book to delve into the technical considerations of style. Little can be said that is not already said in this extraordinary reference. There are, however, some general observations which may be useful, especially for those whose primary expertise lies in other areas.

The conscientious writer with a deep appreciation of the importance of style, but without the extended technical training necessary to achieve all of the objectives involved, is often exposed to a subtle creative trap. He begins, often subconsciously, to worry so much about the rules of grammar, punctuation, and the like—partly from a fear of looking foolish, uneducated, or unprofessional—that his creativity begins to be stifled. When this happens it can become a tragedy of major dimensions.

It should always be remembered that there are writers, there are editors, and there are manuals of style—*but one is not the other*! No great book was ever created by a manual of style, however valuable. Few professional editors, however magnificent, have also been truly great writers. Writing is a creative process which, however improved by mechanics and technique, transcends them all and must never be bound by their chains.

Certainly, every serious writer should continue to expand his knowledge of his language. Words are the tools of his trade, the bridge of his communication, and the more effectively he can use them the better. Obviously, he should continue to study and benefit from all available material on acceptable style. But he must *always be the master, never the servant, of the rules.*

As stated in the preface of *A Manual of Style*, 'When style rules go beyond their role of achieving clarity and consistency, when they become precious or merely doctrinaire, they must be changed or eliminated. . . . where no question of good taste or good logic is involved, deference should be shown to the expressed wishes of the author.'

Writers everywhere will applaud those brave words. Yet one finds, again and again, rules that are precious, that do defy logic—even in *A Manual of Style*. As with other absurdities of language, especially in spelling and pronunciation, the writer can, if he chooses, spend a lifetime 'tilting at windmills,' or he can learn to live with them as harmoniously as possible.

Whatever else may be forgotten or ignored, however, the twin objectives of style—clarity and consistency—must remain inviolable.

Editing for production involves design and production decisions which are necessary for the transference of the typed manuscript into typeset form, and the communication of those decisions to the book printer and typesetter. The process initially involves questions of book design—discussed in Chapter 4—that are then interpreted into layouts and formalized typographic instructions. One of the best books available on this subject is titled *Bookmaking: The Illustrated Guide to Design and Production*, written by Marshall Lee and published by R. R. Bowker Company. This excellent book is highly recommended to every author/publisher for their personal library.

After all design questions have been resolved, the manuscript must then be marked to convey the necessary instructions to the typesetter and paging artist in a clear and accurate manner which allows no opportunity for misinterpretation.

Marking a manuscript for production includes the following instructions: type family, face, size, leading, line length, maximum number of text lines per page, indentions, quadding (flush left, right, or centered), second leading (if used), capitalization instructions, and other matters of book design.

It is not necessary to mark every chapter where the instruction is applicable to establish the pattern to be followed.

The basic markings includes type size, leading, and line length. Instructions for the use of 9 point type with a 2 point leading between lines set on a 26 pica line would be marked 9/11 x 26. (The basic point size and leading are *added together* to establish the total leading amount.)

Indents are usually marked with squares, positioned at the spot of indention. One square indicates a 1 em indent, the numeral 2 in a square means a 2 em indent, etc. Quadding instructions are indicated by brackets as follows:

[Set line flush left

] Set line to the center [

Set line flush right]

Proofreading

After your manuscript is typeset, you will be provided with at least two opportunities, and sometimes three, to proofread your material for typographic errors: *galley proof, page proof*, and press-ready *blueline proof*. (Some book printers, on very large and very special jobs, will also provide a fold-down proof of printed pages directly from the press before sending the job to bindery.) The galley and page proofs will be duplicated copies of the type; the originals of the type will be held by the printer for later corrections.

Proofreading is an important responsibility. It should be done thoroughly and carefully by *two people*—one reading from the original manuscript while the second checks the proof copy. (It is almost impossible for any writer to accurately proofread his own material alone. He tends to 'read in' errors and omissions.) Circle all errors and indicate the correction directly opposite in the margin, using a colored, fine-tip pen or pencil.

The book printer will correct all *printer's errors* (P/E) called to his attention at the galley proof stage at no charge. However, errors not caught until the page proof or blueline stage become progressively more expensive and additional charges may be made.

Most book printers perform only cursory proofreading of galleys before sending them to clients. Like all things involving time, comprehensive in-house proofreading costs money, which, directly or indirectly, must be recovered. Some book printers have typesetters who are so accurate that they and their clients agree, in advance, to bypass in-house proofreading and to pass on the saving to the client. The theory is that the author is going to have to proof the material anyway, so why pay the additional charges involved? Whichever course is followed, the author is totally responsible for finding and noting errors. Regardless of who may have proofed the material previously, it must be proofread by the author as though for the very first time.

Sometimes self-publishers become impatient with the time required for proofreading and want to bypass one or more of the proofreading stages. *This is a very dangerous practice.* The various proofs are for the mutual protection of both parties, and to assure that the final job is perfect, or as nearly perfect as humanly possible. When an author insists on waiving a proof the book printer must have a written release that relieves him from the liability for errors that *might* have been caught at that proof stage.

Production will not proceed on your book until each proof has been read, corrected, signed and returned, so it is to everyone's advantage to do so promptly.

Author's Alterations. Author's alterations (A/A) are changes in textual matter which differ from the original material or instructions furnished, which are requested by the author, publisher or others, and are chargeable by the book printer to the client in addition to original prices quoted.

No book printer *enjoys* charging for author's alterations. They can be a real sore spot and can upset otherwise harmonious relationships. Some printers simply avoid the problem by increasing their original typesetting prices 25 percent or so to compensate for costs which *may* occur from this problem. However, this practice unduly penalizes those clients who conscientiously edit and correct their manuscripts to avoid such problems. Discuss author's alterations with your book printer. If you want him to guarantee no author's alteration charges he will probably be willing to adjust his price accordingly.

Every author wants his final product to be as complete, well-worded, logically organized, and produced as professionally as possible—and properly so. From the time his material is presented for typesetting to the time he sees it in typeset form, new facts and observations present themselves, and new and fresher thoughts flash through his creative mind.

There is, therefore, a terrible temptation—even a compulsion, sometimes—to endlessly alter copy at every proofing stage. And there are, of course, occasional changes that are so crucial to the objectives of the author that they *must* be made, regardless of cost. Book printers understand and empathize with the reasons for author's alterations, and will make them at any proofing stage as required.

But it is also important that authors understand, in advance, that such alterations are *terribly costly*. The alteration of a single word can frequently cost more than an entire paragraph. Additions and deletions that are made after copy has been paged may mean reshuffling many pages, in addition to the cost of resetting the type. Changes at the blueline stage mean new negatives, new paging, and new type—a prohibitively costly procedure.

Your book printer is as anxious as you that your book be a professional representation of your efforts, *and of his.* But when such alterations are the result of a lack of thoroughness in editing the original manuscript, the high costs that must be passed on are hard to justify. *The time to study and correct your manuscript is before it has been typeset.*

Most book printers maintain a special job cost account for the accumulation of time spent by all production personnel on author's alterations. This account is posted directly from employee's time cards, usually on a daily basis. When a job is completed, all such time will be charged, in addition to prices quoted, at the printer's 'standard hourly rates' for the work done.

Proofreaders' Marks. The proofreaders' marks that follow are accepted as standard by the typographers in this country and in most foreign countries. You should use them when checking proofs.

The marks of punctuation

⊙ Period

⋀ or ⁹⁄ Comma

=/ or -/ Hyphen

:/ Colon

;/ Semicolon

⋁⁹ Apostrophe

!/ Exclamation mark or Exclamation point

?/ Question mark or Interrogation point

| en | or $\frac{1}{en}$ En dash

| em | or $\frac{1}{em}$ One em dash

| 2 em | or $\frac{2}{em}$ Two em dash

( ) or (|) Parentheses

⋁⋁ Quotation marks (double)

⋁⋁ Quotation marks (single)

The marks of typography

ℭ Delete or take out

ℭ Delete and close up

stet Let it stand "as is" or disregard changes marked

⋀ Caret: insert

∿ or ⊓ Transpose

tr Marginal symbol for transpose

⟳→ Transfer circled matter to position shown by arrow

⤸ Turn over (letter or cut upside down)

wf Wrong font

ⓧ or ✗ Replace broken or defective letter

Insert space

⌒ Close up space

✓ Equalize space

⎕ Indent one em or insert one em quad

²⎕ Two ems

⁋ Paragraph

no⁋ No paragraph

⊏ Move to left

⊐ Move to right

⊐⊏ Center

⊓ Move up

⊔ Move down

// Align

|| Straighten or justify

lc or *l.c.* Lower case

ital or Scott Italic

bf or Scott Boldface

caps or Scott Capital letters

s.c. or Scott Small capitals

c + s.c. or Scott Caps and small caps

rom Roman (change from italic to roman)

sp Spell out

(?) Query to author

out s.c. Out, see copy

⤸ No paragraph - run in

ld Insert 2 point lead

↓ or ⊥ Push down space

✳ Asterisk

³⋁ Superior figure or letter

⋀₃ Inferior figure or letter

Chapter 4

Typography & Book Production

Typography is the style, arrangement, or appearance of typeset matter. There are now four basic typesetting methods: hot type, strike-on cold type, phototype-setting, and laser printing. Hot type is by far the oldest and involves, in many variations, the use of raised metal characters which are coated with ink and pressed directly against the paper to be printed. Strike-on cold type operates on the principle of the typewriter with raised metal characters on keys or balls which impact onto an inked ribbon, transferring the image to a page which can be photographed. Phototype-setting involves the transmission of a photographic image onto sensitized photographic paper or film. Laser printing, somewhat similar to xerography in final appearance but of much higher quality, applies images to paper from 'type fonts' which are actually contained in computer software programs.

Computerized phototypesetting is a highly sophisticated blending of the technologies of typography, computer science, and phototypesetting. The discussion that follows will be restricted to computerized phototypesetting and laser printing, which are the methods most commonly used today.

How Phototypesetting Works

If you were to hand-print the letters of the alphabet in black ink onto white paper and then photograph those letters with a home camera, you would end up with a negative. The letters would be clear and the rest of the negative would be black, or at least dark. If you were then to position your negative, letter by letter, onto a piece of chemically sensitized photographic paper, exposing each letter to a directed and confined light source, you could form a word. Finally, you could develop your sensitized paper in a photographic developing solution, fix it, wash it, and dry it, and you would see your word reproduced in black on a white paper background.

Using far more precise techniques and equipment, this is the same basic principle used, until recently, in phototypesetting.

Typographic artists draw every character with which the typographer is concerned, precisely positioned and to a very large scale. They then photograph those characters with special cameras, reducing their size to a small fraction of the original. The resulting negative becomes a *type font* from which photographic copies can be made. In some phototypesetting processes, usually restricted to display type, the fonts are made in the form of long strips of negatives and used in a typesetting machine which enables the typesetter to position and expose one character at a time onto photographic paper, thereby forming strips of words. With other processes, these fonts (negatives) are attached to plastic or glass disks which may either be turned manually or mechanically.

While either of these methods may be satisfactory when small amounts of large-size type are involved, they are not practical when massive amounts of text type must be produced at rates of thousands of lines of type per hour.

Computerized Phototypesetting

Typographic equipment designers recognized that, for the phototypesetting principle to be economical and useful in the area of text typography, the operations involved would have to be controlled by some form of high speed mechanism. Not only must the type font move rapidly for the selection of individual characters, but the photographic image of each character must move from side to side across the page and the sensitized paper must move vertically at precise intervals to avoid one line being reproduced on top of the preceding line. Also, characters must be set in more than one type size and face from each font disk; spacing between lines, line lengths, and other typographic requirements must be variable and controlled by automatic command. Most important, the highly complex mathematical computations required for anticipating line lengths and character counts, so that each line may be justified (straight right and left margins), must be made in fractions of a second.

To achieve these very sophisticated objectives, phototypesetters were equipped with a built-in computer which reproduced type photographically onto continuous rolls of sensitized paper from type disks containing several rows or faces of type. Type characters were photographically enlarged through command-controlled lenses to virtually any type size desired. The exposed sensitized paper was then automatically fed into a light-tight holding cassette and then through an automatic developing processor, after which galleys of type were paged and photographed for printing.

As both laser, graphics, and computer technologies became more sophisticated, they were combined for further improvements in state-of-the-art phototypesetters. Today, instead of using negative fonts, the design of each character is actually programmed into the computer software. And, instead of enlarging or reducing the image through lenses, those images are projected, without distortion, onto the chemically treated paper by laser beams.

Computerized typesetters are designed to utilize the principle of 'total command.' This means that all typographic instructions (type family, size, face, line length, leading, quadding, justification, leaders, indents, runarounds, etc.) can be set on disks at input terminals by the typesetter. Once set, the output device will carry out all necessary typographic functions automatically and without further instruction.

The keyboard on a typographer's input terminal is similar to electronic typewriter keyboards, but there are many important differences and additions. A typewriter usually has only two characters available for each key—upper case (capitals) and lower case. Since most typewriters have forty-four keys, this means that the typist is normally limited to a total of eighty-eight characters.

Professional typesetters must have a much wider range of characters, including a full range of fractions, squares, bullets, small capitals, etc. To provide for these special symbol needs, input keyboards are equipped with what is, in effect, a third row of keys, sometimes called a supershift position. These extra symbol positions often vary depending on the type family being used. Special combinations are available for general job typography, book typography, and others, with each offering special symbols commonly required by that particular industry. Foreign language disks or fonts are also available.

Input terminal keyboards are equipped with special function panels which enable the operators to embed typographic codes for line length, point size, primary leading, secondary leading, dot leaders, rules, etc.

Typesetting From Personal Computers

With the widespread use of personal computers, continuing advances have been made in their use as input terminals for phototypesetting. At the most elementary level, computers can be used as 'dumb' terminals simply to capture keystrokes and thereby avoid the time, costs, and errors inherent in rekeyboarding text by the typesetter. Since keyboarding manuscripts on a typesetter constitutes from 30 to 40 percent of the typesetting charge, significant savings are obviously possible from this technique alone.

Every personal computer has its own special 'language.' So does every phototypesetter. Since these languages are different, some form of translation is necessary. The common language most often used for such translations is called *hexidecimal.*

Several 'black boxes' are now on the market which allow such three-stage translations to be made. One of the more popular is manufactured by The Shaftstall Corporation and is called the MediaCom. It not only makes the basic translations required, but it also has a system of arrays which allow the typesetter to make special character conversions.

With the general acceptance of the IBM PC compatibles as the 'standard' within the personal computer industry, conversions from such compatibles have become routine. Conversions can also be made from non-compatible computers, but additional costs are usually involved.

In typesetter's terms, computer keyboards are relatively simplistic. For example, there are no right and left quote marks—all quote marks are inch marks. There is also no key to call for ems, ens, bullets, boxes, and dozens of other requirements which are common in professional typesetting.

The MediaCom array system allows the typesetter to embed customized instructions which say, in effect, that when the system reads a 'Space-Inch' character combination, that combination will be translated into a 'Left Quote' character; when it reads an 'Inch-Space' character combination, that combination will be translated into a 'Right Quote' character. Almost any number of such translations can be customized for the special needs of clients.

One of the most common typographic commands is used at the end of each paragraph. When text is being set in justified mode, a special quad left-return command must be issued on the last line of each paragraph to force all type on those lines to the left. If this is not done, the typesetter will attempt to 'spread' the words and characters from the right to the left margin in an effort to 'justify' it. If additional space is required between paragraphs which is less or greater than a standard 'double space,' a secondary leading command must also be issued. Finally, if the first line of the next paragraph is to be indented, one or more em, en, or fixed spaces must be entered.

As simple as these commands are, when not using a typesetting keyboard, they can become irksome and time-consuming for the author/computer operator.

There are two ways around this. At the end of each paragraph, pseudo-typographic commands can be inserted on the computer which are translated into 'real' typographic commands by the Mediacom. While any number of codes can be used, our own company uses the dollar sign followed by alpha characters. Since no one would want to type out such codes at the end of each paragraph, they can be stored to a glossary name in the word processor, such as 'L.' Then, at the end of each paragraph, the glossary named 'L' can be called for, which will insert as the full code array.

While this method works, it can become confusing. It also makes editing computer hardcopy more tedious.

There is an easier technique which involves consistent spacings between paragraphs, heads, sub-heads, etc. If two spaces are consistently allowed between paragraphs, the MediaCom arrays can be customized to read those spaces exactly as though they were typograhic codes, and to instruct the typesetter accordingly.

When word processsing software is used in preparing manuscripts for typesetting conversion, the manuscript should not be formatted with the word processor's formatting capabilities and 'hard' returns should not be used except at the ends of paragraphs. (Use your word wrap capabilities instead.)

When you save and copy your disk, convert it to unformatted ASCII. With MicroSoft Word, for example, this can be done by simply saying 'No' to the formatting question when the disk is saved.

Teletypesetting

While direct, disk-to-disk conversions are most common, manuscripts can also be 'dumped' over the telephone lines to the special number which your typesetter can furnish to you. This will require that you have a modem and communications software. One of the more popular modems is the Hayes 2400 SuperModem which can send data at speeds up to 2400 Baud. One of the more popular and worry-free communication software packages is called CrossTalk.

The big advantage of teletypesetting is that it saves the time that would otherwise be involved in mailing or delivering your disk to your typesetter. The disadvantage is that it may involve significant long distance telephone charges, unless you are dealing with a local typesetter. It is important that you also send a hardcopy of your manuscript to your typesetter to avoid any possible confusion or misunderstandings.

Electronic Pagination

Until recently, most books were paginated using the cut-and-paste method, with either rubber cement or adhesive hot wax. This meant that type was first reproduced in galleys, sent to clients for proofreading and correction, then cut apart with scissors and layed up on pre-printed layout pages.

Like all manual activities, however, this method was both slow and costly. This was especially true when the format involved running heads, footnotes, illustrations, multiple columns, etc. Such jobs could easily involve six or more laydowns per page, at a cost of about $1.00 or more per laydown. Being a manual operation, it also introduced the problem of keeping all of the elements on the page straight and true with other elements.

With computers, and the very sophisticated pagination software now available, programs can be developed which paginate such jobs automatically, thereby eliminating the need for galleys and galley proofs.

This technology not only reduces pagination time and costs very significantly, but it also makes last-minute revisions less troublesome.

The problem with this approach is that the cost of developing the original programs involved can be significant, meaning that maximum cost savings only occur on larger jobs. It also means that manuscripts simply *must* be provided in a totally professional and complete manner. When they are not, the benefits of such an approach are not only lost, but actual cost penalties may be incurred.

Computer Graphics

A spinoff of electronic pagination technology is the introduction of computer graphics into the pagination process. Today, both line and continuous tone illustrations can be scanned by optical scanners and stored, in digitized forms, on computer disks. Once in this form, they can then be manipulated in almost any way desired. They can be enlarged, reduced, slanted, cropped or altered. They can also be interfaced with the text, which is also stored on disks, to produce a final, paginated book in either negative or positive form.

Positive Halftones & Direct-Imaging Platemakers

While not as technologically sophisticated as some of the electronic scanning systems now available—but usually much more time- and cost-effective—computerized positive halftone cameras are now available which produce high quality halftones from continuous tone photographs at savings up to 50 percent compared to other methods. No negatives are involved, which means the elimination of rubyliths, halftone negatives, and manual strip-ins—a very time-consuming bottleneck in book production. This system also offers the advantage of providing the client with a high quality, final, positive page proof with all illustrations in place and 'viewable.'

An important companion to such a 'positive' system is the new, large-press direct-image platemaker which allows printing plates to be made directly from camera-ready copy on large templates, without the time and cost involved in producing plate-ready negatives.

Desktop Publishing

The latest, and most popular, addition to the world of typesetting and publishing is desktop publishing.

It was first introduced by the Apple Computer Company utilizing the McIntosh computer, the laser writer, and Aldous Desktop Publishing Software. Some time later, Xerox Corporation brought out the Ventura Desktop Publishing

Software which could be used on IBM PC Compatible computers with the Hewitt-Packard Laser Printer.

Both of these systems perform extraordinary pagination feats, and involve relatively low initial investments (in comparison to comparable results from phototypesetting systems). Complete systems can be purchased for less than $10,000. While the two systems vary somewhat in approach, the results from each are similar, the final quality being largely dependent on the d.p.i. (dots per inch) availability of the laser printer being used.

The biggest problem that both face, at this writing, lies in the low print-out resolution of most existing laser printers (300 to 600 d.p.i.). However, resolutions are being increased to 1200 dots and higher.

As with all new technologies, there are limitations. While the quality is good, it is still far below that commonly available from phototypesetters. There are also restrictions in type fonts, families, faces, and size availabilities, primary and secondary leadings between lines and paragraphs, special symbols, etc.

When realistic time and hourly rate standards are applied, the savings are rarely as much as enthusiastic users like to believe.

In spite of such problems, however, desktop publishing technology brings an entirely new and important dimension to book and manual typesetting and pagination. It is especially important for publishers of short-run manuals and books which would otherwise have had to be produced in camera-ready form from typewriter originals, which certainly includes cookbooks, family histories, technical manuals, etc.

Typographic Design Considerations

The typographic design of your book will have a major influence on its beauty and readability, and will be a significant factor in reader enjoyment. Type set with lines that are too long, too close together, or in too small a type size diminishes reader comfort and pleasure—often without really understanding the cause of this subtle irritation. Type with broken or fuzzy letters, or set in an unpleasing face, immediately downgrades your book in the eyes of professional booksellers and readers alike, and is an insult to the time and effort you have invested in your work.

Most modern book specialists attempt to provide the most sophisticated phototypesetting facilities currently available. They usually have dozens of type families and faces from which to choose, resulting in a typographic design that will harmonize and support the art inherent in your material.

Composition is defined as 'the setting of type characters to form words, phrases and sentences for subsequent printing.' Typography is defined as 'the art of selecting, arranging and setting type; the study of printing from type characters; the appearance or arrangement of printed matter.'

While there is an inevitable overlapping between the two approaches, it is fair to say that the basic approach of composition is mechanistic, whereas the objectives of typography, while certainly including all mechanical considerations, extend beyond them to the aesthetics of design and the subtleties of effective communication.

If the only objective of an author were the presentation of words, facts, and data on a take-it-or-leave-it basis, it could be achieved as well, at much lower cost, by using handwriting or a typewriter. But this is rarely the case. Few manuscripts are such sought-after pearls of wisdom that readers will take time from their busy schedules to dig out and decipher a message that is presented tediously.

People are people—and authors, publishers, and typographers must recognize and accept them as they are, not as they perhaps should be. The time available for reading, for all of us, is limited and precious, and becoming more so every day. We are inundated with newspapers, magazines, journals, books, and reports which we *should* read. We are overwhelmed with information from radio and television that captures us as reluctant prisoners, if we are to receive the other enjoyments of their carefully calculated mix.

There is simply not enough time for it all, so readers either 'turn off' completely or else become highly selective to such efforts at communication with which they are confronted.

Any effort to get a message read, comprehended, supported, and acted upon, in today's reader market, requires all the skill, psychological insight, and graphic art that can be mustered. Nowhere is this more true than in the area of typography, and nowhere in typography is it more relevant than in the field of books, which normally involves large quantities of often complex material to be communicated.

The overriding objective of typography is to get the message read and understood, as pleasantly as possible. The achievement of this objective calls for a realistic understanding and appreciation of the needs of your readers. While there is, admittedly, a vast amount of research needed in this important area, some facts are known:

Disorganized Presentations. Readers do not like confused, disorganized material, and few will take the time to restructure such presentations in their own minds. They *do* appreciate and respond to highly organized, building-block presentations which—point by point, idea by idea—build upon, reinforce, and extend that which preceded in a logical, credible way to lead toward specific intellectual or emotional objectives.

The primary responsibility for such presentations is obviously the author's. However, if the author has adhered to such a concept, typographers can recognize it, accentuate it, and artistically present it in a manner that strengthens the author's intentions.

Unbroken Masses of Type. Except in the case of novels and stories—in which readers become active, emotional participants in the drama being unfolded—readers do not like endless, foreboding, unbroken masses of type. A reader tends to subconsciously review printed material in advance and to make judgments of the amount of time and energy he will have to invest to reach the end. If the investment appears to be too great, he may simply skip it.

Whenever possible, type should be arranged in digestible, inviting 'chunks,' separated by a liberal sprinkling of white space, paragraphs, chapters, illustrations, etc.

Long Lines of Type. Readers dislike long lines of type. They are difficult to read, tiring to the eyes, and psychologically challenging. It is generally felt that line lengths of twenty-four picas or less (about four inches) are probably the most readable. When longer lines are necessary they should be combined with larger sizes of type and greater leading between lines.

Small Type. Readers resent small type, and many cannot see well enough to read it easily. But even when they can, type smaller than 9 points is difficult to read, hard on—and possibly damaging to—the eyes, tiring, and generally irritating. Conversely, type that is too large may also have pitfalls in that some readers may feel they are reading material for children or that the publisher is trying to 'fill' a book, and be turned off because of it.

Depending on the amount of copy involved, line length, leading, and type face, type sizes of 10 or 11 points are generally ideal. Footnotes and other reference material not intended for the general reader may be safely set in 7 or 8 point type, if the line length is not too long. Short copy groups may go up to 12 points for special emphasis but seldom much larger.

Leading. The amount of white space allowed between lines is called leading (pronounced 'leding'). Type with no leading is said to be 'set solid.'

The use of liberal amounts of leading serves the same purpose as the use of white space and makes the message appear less tedious and more inviting. It also increases readability and reduces reading fatigue.

In printers' terminology, one vertical inch is equal to 72 points. The minimum acceptable amount of leading is generally 1 point. The ideal leading between lines is probably 2 points. Under some conditions (especially with very long lines and large type sizes) as much as 3 points may be used, but seldom more. However, the mechanical necessities of copyfitting may sometimes have to take precedence over these ideals.

When we speak of leading we normally mean the 'primary leading' between lines of text type. There is also a 'secondary leading,' however, which is usually greater than the primary leading but less than a full double space. It is often used between paragraphs and copy groups.

Type Styles. The selection of type styles or families to be used is largely a matter of preference, tradition, and economy. There is little hard evidence to prove that one is a great deal more acceptable than another.

The primary choice is whether to use a serif or a sans serif type. Serif types have a short cross-line or 'tick' at the ends of the stroke of a Roman letter; sans serifs do not. Most sans serif types are more narrow in character width than comparable sizes and styles of type with serifs. This means more characters per line and less pages in a book, which can often save money. In spite of this, most books are produced with a serif type, mainly because they are felt to be less mechanistic and more aesthetically pleasing on a full page. Sans serif types are usually used for statistical data due to their clear and precise numeric design.

Book Design

At its most elementary level, a book consists of a certain number of blank pages which can be filled with text or copy. At such a level there is little problem with or room for design considerations.

As the objectives for a book shift further and further away from reference or compulsory reading toward areas of persuasion, or attempts at higher levels of reader interest, understanding, and enjoyment, design considerations become increasingly important.

Paging Formats. There are hundreds of possible variations in page design. Some are good; others are not so good.

Most of us have a natural propensity to be different from the ordinary. If we are artistically or creatively inclined, we want to say things in a different way, and to present our thoughts in a new and fresh manner. We tire of the traditional approaches and long for the untried, the unspoiled, and the unusual. Unfortunately, however, if one is not a professional or experienced book designer, 'uniqueness' can sometimes turn into a costly and unpleasant production tragedy. *Off-size books*, that do not fit standard press sizes, can often *double* production costs. Books bound on the short side may sometimes have disastrous practical and production consequences. Irregular and seemingly attractive typographic designs can significantly increase typesetting costs and triple pagination costs. All of which may well be worth the investment—provided the consequences are clearly understood, in advance, and are acceptable. For those who are perhaps a little less adventurous and who must present their material effectively and attractively—but within a budget—some book specialists maintain standing page formats which have been tested and proven over many years of book production. They are usually attractive, well-balanced, provide for an ample amount of white space. They fit their presses and their paper manufacturers' standards, and they 'work.' Equally important, preprinted paging sheets are usually available for all of them, and they can reduce pagination costs (and your price) significantly.

Through the advance selection of one of these page formats you are automatically deciding on a full range of pre-established specifications which you know to be completely acceptable. They include: page size, line measure, column height, maximum number of lines per page, margins (top, bottom, and sides) running heads, and page number positioning. You know, in advance, what your page will look like. After you select the type family, size, and leading you will also know the maximum number of characters you can expect a page to accommodate. You can then accurately calculate total page count for your book based on a character count of your manuscript.

Page Size. Most books are produced in one of the following page sizes, with the binding on the longest side: 4½" x 7", 4" x 9", 5½" x 8½", 6" x 9", and 8½" x 11". Less popular sizes include 7" x 10" and 9" x 12". However, any book can be trimmed to a size smaller than the sizes shown. For example, a 5½" x 8½" book can be trimmed to 5" x 8". There will usually be no penalty involved in going to a smaller than standard size, but there will also be no saving.

From the standpoint of design, it is easier to develop an attractive page with larger page sizes than with smaller ones, although the 6" x 9" size is usually a good compromise. However, functional considerations may have to play a greater role than aesthetics in the selection of a page size. If a book is destined to be placed in a catalog rack or file drawer by the user, the 8½" x 11" size may be the most appropriate. Or if the user is likely to carry the book in a purse or pocket, the 5½" x 8½" size (or smaller) is probably more desirable.

Under some circumstances, design and content suggest the standard size increments, but with the binding edge on the shortest side. While this can be very attractive, you should check with your book printer in advance to see if it involves special production problems.

Many quality paperbacks, hardback books, and novels designed for general reader markets use the 6" x 9" size. It is economical, attractive, and easy to hold and read. Books with dramatic art or photography will often require the 9" x 12" size to provide the most pleasing presentation. Mass-market paperbacks are standardized on the 4¼" x 7" size, which fits the large, high-speed web and belt presses used for such books. Display racks used by retailers for these books are also standardized on this size. While very economical in long runs (100,000 and over), the economy is lost when moderate or small quantities are produced.

White Space. Some author/publishers want to fill every square inch of white space with copy. Otherwise, they feel, they are paying for an area that says nothing, produces nothing, and is an extravagant waste.

Nothing could be further from the truth. A generous amount of white space, well-balanced against copy and illustrations, is frequently the best investment that can be made in book printing. Most readers dislike too much copy presented with too heavy a hand. One glance at a page makes it seem to be an endless journey which will require all of their energy to complete. Their subconscious longs for an oasis of visual relief. If it isn't available, and if the copy is not heavily dosed with sex, violence, or suspense, they may simply pass it by.

The liberal use of white space is an important technique for making each page less foreboding, more readable and inviting to the reader. Wide margins—top, bottom, and side, extra sinkage at chapter beginnings, extra space between paragraphs and sections, and extra leading between lines of type are all methods of utilizing white space to hold interest.

Obviously such techniques increase cost and must be weighed against the advantages. Usually they are an excellent investment.

Page Count. The total number of pages that will be required for your book will be determined by (1) the content to be included (text, pictures, graphs, etc.), (2) the page size selected, and (3) the page format to be used, which will determine the amount of white space, margins, type size, leading between lines of type, type styles, and line lengths.

In printing terminology, *a page is one side of one sheet in a book. A sheet is considered to be two pages.*

Blank pages are also counted as pages since they are basically processed as though they had printing on them.

Books are printed on large size sheets called 'signatures' which are then folded to the pre-trim size of the final book. Books that consist of even signature increments (i.e., 16, 32, or 64 pages) are the most economical to produce.

Often, however, this involves too many blank pages. The next most economical increment is a half-signature. If this still involves too many blanks they can, at some premium, be produced as quarter 'sigs.' Actually, the cost involved in using quarter-sigs is often as much or more than half-sigs. The advantage is that blanks are reduced or eliminated.

It is important that the final number of pages be known, at least approximately, before type is set or layout is commenced. The book printer must also know your feelings in regard to budget versus design, and the amount of leeway and judgment he is to be allowed. If he *must* fit your manuscript into a selected number of pages, then he will make every possible effort to do so. But something (type size, leading, margins, etc.) may have to be sacrificed.

The only way that total page count can be computed in advance, with any degree of accuracy, is to have your entire manuscript available at one time and at the beginning. Manuscripts must be professionally prepared and typed to a consistent average line length with the same number of lines per full page. There must be no miscellaneous inserts and bits of paper to be stuck in, and all pictures and other illustrations must be provided.

Even with all of this, however, advance calculations of final page count are subject to unavoidable change due to unique paging and design considerations which may be encountered as pagination progresses. It should be understood, therefore, that the page count indicated in the book printer's quotation is only his best estimate of that which will be required. When layout or pagination requirements result in a different final page count, price and production adjustments will have to be made, usually in eight page increments.

While copyfitting is normally a complex activity—involving character count, line lengths, and line number computations—with the use of standard page formats it becomes relatively simple, even for the novice.

Once a format, type size, and leading have been selected, the total 'character equivalent' capacity of a full typeset page can be determined by simply reading the table that is usually at the bottom of each format illustration. When manuscripts have been typed as recommended, with a one inch margin on all four sides, it is easy to determine the total character equivalent count per full typewritten manuscript page. If the manuscript has been typed with an elite typewriter, which sets twelve characters per inch, and the average line length is 6½″, this results in an average of 78 typewriter characters per line. Since double spaced typewriting usually results in 3 horizontal lines per vertical inch, a 9″ column (11″ — 2″) allows for 27 lines per page. The total number of lines (27) multiplied by the average number of characters per line (78) gives the total character equivalent per manuscript page—2,106 characters. (Pica typewriter should be computed based on ten characters per inch or 65 characters per 6½″ line. This computes to 1,755 characters per full manuscript page.)

By multiplying the number of manuscript full-page equivalents for each chapter by the typewriter character equivalents per full manuscript page, and dividing the total number of characters by the typeset page character capacity shown for the format selected, the final number of full pages per chapter can be determined. To this total must be added an allowance for 'sinkage' at the beginning of, and partial pages at the end of, each chapter, front material, back material, illustrations, etc.

While the final page count calculation may not be completely accurate, it should be close enough for preliminary considerations.

All computations are based on character equivalents. Each line is considered to be *fully typed or set.* Heads and subheads are counted as full lines of type. Every key stroke (spaces, commas, etc.) is counted as one character.

Illustrations. Some books, by the nature of their message, do not require illustrations. Others, however, are so pictorially oriented, or so complex, that pictures, drawings, and charts are essential for maximum reader comprehension and appreciation.

One small, carefully chosen picture or drawing can convey, at a glance, an explanation that would require far greater space with words alone. Some explanations, especially those involving complicated instructions, are hard to follow without supporting how-to illustrations.

In addition to the obvious functional uses of illustrations, they also break the monotony of continuing, straight-text matter and create a far less challenging atmosphere for those who hate to read anyway.

From a printing standpoint, there are two kinds of pictures. One is called a line picture, such as you would draw with a pen. The other is called a continuous tone picture (later converted to a halftone positive or negative), which is the kind of picture you might produce with a home camera.

Line pictures—drawn in black ink, to size, and without tonal shading—present no problem to the printer and involve no significant cost penalties. They are simply applied, at any desired location, on the page paste-up along with any accompanying text type, and photographed with the rest of the page. However, if they are drawn in pencil or in color, or if they must be reduced or enlarged to fit, then veloxes will have to be made, at some additional cost.

Continuous tone pictures are another matter. They must be sized, photographed separately from the rest of the page, a 'dot structure' must be introduced by use of a special screen, a rubylith window must be cut and applied to the paste-up, and the halftone negative must be trimmed and applied to the basic page negative. The additional cost involved for each individual picture can be significant. With proper planning, however, substantial cost reductions can be achieved.

Such savings depend primarily on two factors: the similarity of contrast between the original photographs and whether the originals involved will be photographed at the same percentage of reduction or enlargement. For example, if four 4″ x 6″ black-and-white photographs of similar contrast are to be reduced to a single common size (i.e., 2″ x 3″), they can all be processed together, using a 50 percent reduction, and costs are greatly reduced. But if one is an 8″ x 10″ color portrait, the second is a 2″ x 2″ snapshot with little contrast, and so forth, and all must print the same size, then they must be processed one-by-one.

Sizing Illustrations. When illustrations are to be used, the originals will often be oversize and must be 'sized' to determine the reduction percentage that is necessary to bring them down (or up) to the desired final size. While it frequently isn't, this information should be available before illustrations are 'cropped.'

When an illustration is photographically reduced or enlarged, *every* dimension alters in exactly the same percentage—vertically, horizontally, and diagonally. For this reason, arbitrary crop marks, made without consideration for layout space availabilities may be very unrealistic.

Picture sizings should always be expressed as *a percent of the original*, which is the reciprocal of the actual reduction required. For example, if an 8" x 10" picture is to be reduced by 30 percent, the sizing instructions written on the back of the picture should read '70 percent,' which means that the picture should be reduced *to* 70 percent. It is also helpful if the actual dimensions desired are computed and included.

When many illustrations must be sized, you may want to purchase a 'reduction wheel.' They are inexpensive and are available at most photographic supply stores.

Special Effects. Special illustrative effects can be achieved through such techniques as reverses, bleeds, and duotones.

A reverse is the alteration of printed images, normally appearing as black or colored on clear paper, to print as clear images or letters surrounded by areas of solid or screened ink. (A printer cannot normally print white ink on dark colored papers.) A bleed is the extension of a printed image beyond the trim edge of the page. A duotone is a halftone printed in two different colors of ink (normally black and one color) from two different sets of negatives and plates.

These and other special illustrative effects can, on occasion, be very useful and attractive. However, when used on inside pages, they usually elevate your book into an entirely different printing cost class, since they can require significant amounts of extra labor to produce.

Makeup Dummy. A 'dummy,' in printer's terminology, is a hand-sketched set of sheets of paper cut and bound, or folded, to indicate the size, shape, sequence, appearance, layout, and contents of a publication to be printed. If your book includes illustrations, charts, or any special formatting you can expedite production considerably by preparing such a dummy to accompany your manuscript.

A dummy doesn't need to be elaborate, and you needn't be an artist to prepare one. Simply take a handful of typing sheets and indicate page-by-page, in pencil, the groups of information that you would *like* to have on each. Pictures and drawings can be indicated by rectangles. If you want a blank page, leave a page blank, and indicate it as such. Number your pages and staple them together. Unless you instruct otherwise, your dummy will be used only as a rough guide and will be revised as necessary, based on your book printer's judgment and the mechanics of production.

Dust Jackets

Hardback books that will be marketed commercially through bookstores should have separate dust jackets. Not only do dust jackets protect the book from soil and damage while the books are on display, but they also provide the same protection while being read, loaned to friends, and on the reader's bookshelf. Equally important, they provide an extraordinarily effective means of adding sales appeal to the book and making it stand out among the hundreds of other books on the retailer's display shelf, against which it must compete for attention. The art work and design, the jacket blurb and flap copy, the picture and biographical sketch about the author, and excerpts from any reviews that may have been made—all help immensely in increasing point-of-sale buyer interest and action.

Camera-Ready Copy

Book printers are sometimes asked to quote prices based on camera-ready copy only to find, after being awarded the contract, that a significant amount of additional processing is required to bring the material to a true camera-ready condition. This can be a real problem when originals have been layed out on oversize illustration board, a common practice with advertising agencies when they are preparing copy for brochures and small booklets. This difference in technique and terminology can create substantial additional costs, which must be paid by someone.

In the manufacture of books it is necessary that large numbers of pages and negatives be processed quickly and efficiently. They simply cannot be handled on a *one-at-a-time* basis. To achieve this objective, originals are photographed in full-signature layouts with all pages mounted side-by-side and head-to-head on special templates which provide for folding, trimming, and page sequence imposition. This technique is impossible when originals are furnished on oversize boards.

Most book printers operate their camera departments on the assumption that all flats can be photographed and developed automatically, at the same camera settings, exposure, and development times, and that no special darkroom compensation techniques will be required at that production stage. If this is not the case, additional processing is required to bring originals to this condition—and negative costs can increase significantly.

Camera-ready jobs are usually quoted on the assumption that (1) all copy has been paged by the client on layout sheets prepared and furnished, or approved by the book printer, (2) all copy is strong, black-on-white, and of velox quality, (3) correctly sized rubylith windows, when required, have been positioned for all halftones, (4) charts, tables, and line drawings have been processed to required size, and are in position, (5) page numbers have been applied, (6) table of contents, the index, and other front and back material, if required, have been completed and paged, (7) cover art and typography is complete and paginated, (8) all required overlays have been positioned, register marks have been applied to all parts, and fit, without additional processing, and (9) bleeds, solids, and screens do not require additional processing.

Additional charges will usually be necessary when any of the above activities must be completed by the book printer to bring a client's copy to an acceptable camera-ready condition.

Typewriter Copy

There are many kinds of books that do not warrant or need printer's type. This is especially true of some books put out by organizations that are intended solely for their own membership. Some associations prepare annual convention reports which are made up of papers presented by their members at the convention. Other groups publish membership directories which must be produced at the lowest possible cost.

When properly handled, books can be produced from typewriter originals or computer hardcopy print outs at enormous savings, and still be very attractive. Not only is the cost of typesetting and pagination eliminated, but other production costs can be reduced through the use of oversize typing sheets.

However, technique is the key. If you plan on doing your own typing for a camera-ready typewritten book, be sure to read the following suggestions carefully.

Contact your book printer *before you start*. Many have preprinted typing sheets which they make available at no charge in any quantity you may need. They are usually on a good grade of paper that produces an excellent typing image, they are cut to exactly the correct size for efficient production, and they will usually have guide lines to tell you exactly where to set your side and top margins. These typing sheets are an important part of the printer's production system and are essential if you are to receive the lowest price possible. They will also make your typing and layout job much easier and faster. *Be sure to use them.*

Use an electric, carbon-ribbon typewriter. If one is not available to you, they can be rented for about $40 per month. A typewriter with the lift-off correcting ribbon is ideal. Typing corrections can also be made with liquid opaque. When you make an error, simply move your carriage and white over the mistake with a thin coat, two coats if necessary. Do not apply thick coats and do not attempt to retype until the correcting fluid is dry.

Manual, cloth-ribbon typewriters are *not satisfactory*. The image is usually irregular, often too light in some places and filled-in in others. Either of these conditions worsen when the material is photographed. This results in an inferior printing job and costs *more* money to produce.

Typing sheets are usually designed for either 5½″ x 8½″ or 6″ x 9″ page sizes. They can be either oversize or same-size. Oversize sheets which allow for a 20 percent reduction are ideal. The resulting image is attractive and easy to read. Best of all, their use means that you can print about the same number of words on a 6″ x 9″ page size that you would otherwise have on an 8½″ x 11″ page size. Press cost can often be cut in half and paper cost will be reduced by about 30 percent. If you are willing to accept a reduction to 5½″ x 8½″ page size, your savings will be even greater.

Computer Hardcopy

Many word processors and laser printers can now format pages and print them in a variety of type faces. Where appropriate, this technique can save a great deal of money by eliminating the cost of printer's type and produce attractive books and manuals in the bargain.

If you use a dot matrix printer, it is very important that you always start your printout with a fresh, new ribbon. If you use a laser printer, be sure that it is in good working order and that you have plenty of toner. Also use a good grade of paper; a No. 1 Bond, if possible.

It's very important that you position every page consistently, especially if you will be publishing a smaller size book, such as 5½″ x 8½″ or 6″ x 9″. Your book printer will probably gang-cut your letter-size originals down to the final trim size of your book so that they can be layed up on templates.

Ad Copy

Many organizations include ads in their books to help defray costs or to serve as a fund-raising project. This can be a very profitable activity for any organization, when it is handled properly.

If your book contains ads it is essential that you consult with your book printer in advance of ad sales so he can provide you with the proper ad layout forms, type samples, and procedures to follow. Prices for typesetting ads will usually assume that such an approach will be followed. If it isn't, your printer's cost (and your price) can easily increase. And what should have been a relatively simple, highly organized activity can turn into a production disaster that will almost certainly extend beyond the promised delivery deadline.

Here is one workable system for handling ads:

1. All ads must be prepared and submitted on ad layout sheets furnished by the printer, using one ad per sheet.

2. Each ad must be sequentially numbered by size. For example, F-1, H-1, Q-1, E-1, etc. for full, half, quarter, and eighth page ads.

3. All type sizes and styles must be selected from the type samples shown on the ad layout sheets, and all selections must be indicated by number on each ad. When numbers are omitted, the printer will use his own best judgment.

4. Pictures, logos, etc., must be attached to the ad sheet for which they will be used.

5. A complete listing, in ad number sequence, must be furnished with ad copy for audit and control.

6. All ads will be prepared on standing ad paging sheets with pre-printed border rulings.

7. Prices are based on the following maximum number of lines per ad. Full page ads—8 lines; half page ads—6 lines; quarter page ads—4 lines; eighth page ads—1 line. Additional lines will be charged as overlines.

8. Ads repeated from previous publications, business cards, letterheads, etc., which do not require resetting in type, should be corner-taped on regular ad forms. Do not put tape on top of the image. Light colors (light yellows, blues, etc.) may not photograph and may have to be reset.

9. Prices do not include art work, special rulings, or special ad formats. Unless specifically stated otherwise, prices do not include halftones, color dropouts, light color restorations, special borders, overlines, or logo enlargements or reductions, for which additional charges will be added.

Paper and Ink

Most books are printed on uncoated book papers. Very high quality books with many photographs and books using full-color will usually be printed on coated book papers. Art-oriented books or those requiring a special aesthetic 'feel' will sometimes be printed on text papers.

Unlike bond papers, book papers are not classified by grade number or rag content. They depend mainly on trade names, coating treatments, and finish for differentiation.

Uncoated offset book papers are available in at least four quality ranges. The most expensive 'grade' will accept half-tones, solids, and line copy well and will be much whiter than the less expensive grades. It is available with special whitening agents which increase its whiteness still further and can also be purchased in an opaque grade.

Some book printers regularly stock acid-free grades of paper in both white and off-white, uncoated only. If so, your costs will not be significantly higher than other comparable grades of paper. Since such papers are free of acid content, they have very good archival qualities and are highly recommended for all books that need a long life expectancy. It is especially desirable for family histories, church histories, etc.

Less expensive grades are progressively less white, less opaque, have shorter life expectancies (archival qualities), and are less expensive. The lowest grade is a form of newsprint, and is often used in mass-marketed paperbacks.

Price differentials between kinds and grades of paper are substantial. Since paper constitutes a major portion of a book's total cost, and has a major effect on the list price which must be charged, a careful balance between quality and price becomes essential.

Weight. Paper is traditionally classified by weight, which also indicates its approximate thickness. To the uninitiated, these weight classifications can be puzzling. For example, a 65 lb. cover paper is much heavier and thicker than 80 lb. offset book paper. The reason is that the paper industry classifies different categories of paper by different base sizes. Offset and text papers are related to the weight of 500 sheets (one ream) of a base size of 25″ x 38″. Cover papers are related to the weight of 500 sheets of a base size of 20″ x 26″.

Since it is seldom practical to actually weigh a single sheet of paper to determine its relative weight, it is usually necessary to rely on a micrometer to check one paper's thickness against similar papers in a paper sample book. While this method works reasonably well, it should be understood that one kind of 60 lb. paper, for example, will not necessarily measure to the same thickness as another with the same weight classification. The varying roller pressures used in their manufacture will often result in different densities, *and* thicknesses. Thicknesses may also vary before and after a paper is printed, as well as from changes in humidity. Smooth finish papers will measure significantly less than the same grade and weight of paper with a vellum finish. The thickness of a coated paper is always much less than a comparable-weight uncoated paper. The reason is that the relatively dense coating, which is applied upon a thinner base paper, is weighed and considered in the weight classification of the coated papers, thereby increasing its weight per inch of thickness.

The thickness of a book is the direct result of both its page count and the thickness of the paper selected. A book can be too thick as well as too thin, not only for reasons of buyer psychology but also because of production considerations. If a book has 600 pages or more, paper that is too thick can create both weight and bindery problems. Uncoated papers in the 50 to 60 lb. range—or a light-weight opaque paper—will probably be required, or, if many halftones are involved, a 50 or 60 lb. *coated* paper may need to be used. At the other extreme, a book with only ninety-six pages may need to be thickened. An 80 lb. weight paper might be used, probably in a high bulk grade.

A paper's opacity must also be considered in relation to the book's content and objectives. Many factors affect opacity other than weight and thickness alone. Coated papers are much more opaque than comparable weights of uncoated papers. Some papers are manufactured in special opaque grades. Aside from these important elements, however, a paper's weight does affect its opacity. An 80 lb. paper is far more opaque, with less 'show through,' than the same paper in a 50 lb. weight. If solids or halftones are to be included this becomes an important factor to be considered.

Balancing all factors, a 60 lb. uncoated paper with a vellum finish is usually a good compromise unless other special requirements are involved.

Finishes. Most offset papers are now available in a wide range of different finishes: smooth, vellum, midi-point, lynn-field embossed, gloss, suede, matte, and others. Whatever finish is selected, the paper itself remains the same since variations in finish are simply the result of a final embossing roll used at the end of the mill run.

Since paper and printing qualities remain essentially the same, finish selection becomes largely a matter of personal choice. A vellum finish, for example, tends to give a softer, richer feel to uncoated papers than smooth finishes. In coated papers there is a strong trend toward the matte or suede finishes and away from the high-gloss finish. Many publishers feel that these velvet-like finishes convey a sense of under-stated, subdued elegance. Most readers also dislike high-gloss finishes due to the problem of light reflecting into the reader's eyes as he reads.

There is no appreciable difference in mill prices for variations in finish. An important point to check, however, is whether your book printer regularly stocks the finish you prefer. If he doesn't, and your job does not require at least a full skid of paper, he may have to buy through his local paper wholesaler since some mills ship in skid lots only. When this is the case, his cost and your price on the paper for your job can easily be increased by 20 to 40 percent, depending on the quantities involved.

Paper Color. It is hard to go wrong with the selection of white paper. It is a highly functional, economical choice that provides maximum legibility and readability. Once a departure is made from this basic selection a brand new set of rules involving personal taste, aesthetics, readability, and function come into play and must be reckoned with.

In recent years paper manufacturers have introduced an avalanche of new and striking paper colors. When effectively harmonized with the total design, ink colors, cover, typography, etc. they can aid in the creation of an attractive and forceful publication. Handled poorly they can create a graphic disaster.

As suggested under 'Finishes,' you should also check with your book printer concerning paper colors. If the color you select is not a standard stock item for him, significant cost penalties may be involved. Aside from this stocking problem, colored paper, on the average, will probably cost 10 to 15 percent more than white. However, this varies by the color selected and the mill supplying it.

Ink Colors. Black ink, like white paper, is hard to beat. It is readable, legible, and universally acceptable. All books that consist mainly of text matter should be printed in black ink. This is especially true for novels, reference, and scholarly books.

This is not to suggest, however, that colored inks may not be desirable under certain special conditions. But colored inks should be used for accent, emphasis, or background in a way that enhances rather than detracts from the basic message. The text portion itself should, almost always, be printed in black ink.

Your book printer has ink selection books (PMS colors) which show hundreds of ink colors from which you may select. It should be remembered, however, that ink colors, when printed, may vary from the samples selected when they are printed on colored paper. Many otherwise bright and dramatic ink colors may appear almost black when printed on deep-tone papers. Even different paper finishes will change the shade of ink. If the sample you selected was printed on a high gloss paper and your job is produced on an uncoated stock, the color can appear to vary by several shades.

The cost of multiple ink colors can have a major effect on the overall price of your book. (Some book manufacturers will not print inside pages in multiple ink colors.) Each ink change involves a charge for press wash-up. Each 'special' color requires a mixing charge. In addition, each color requires an additional set of negatives, additional plates, additional press make-ready and run charges, and additional paper spoilage charges. If close or exact register, or heavy solids, are involved, press runs must be made more carefully and usually at slower speeds.

Bookbinding

Most books are bound in one of four methods: saddle stitch, perfect binding, hardback, or with plastic or wire elements. Saddle stitching involves the use of wire staples (usually two) applied through the fold of the book or booklet. This method of binding is very economical and practical, and is frequently used for books with eighty pages or less. (When books are printed on very light weights of coated paper, page counts of up to 160 pages are sometimes used. However, special presses are required and many book printers will not print on such papers.) While less expensive than other binding methods, it is not as commercially acceptable since there is no spine and the books do not display well in bookstores.

Perfect binding has become the single most popular binding method in use today throughout the book industry. All mass-market paperbacks are perfect bound; quality paperbacks also use this method. It is extremely functional, economical, and allows for a flat spine on which the book's identification can be printed for both bookshelf and display reference. This method is used for books with sixty-four pages or more and can be used up to any reasonable page count.

When used with uncoated inside sheets, and covers that are not coated on the inside surface, there is rarely any problem of sheet separation with normal use. However, covers with coating inside can be a problem and should be carefully considered. Side-stapling may be necessary, as added protection, on very large and thick books which will be exposed to heavy use.

Hardback binding is, of course, the epitome of bookbinding and, while more expensive, cannot be compared to other methods. All quality books that are expected to enjoy a long life and heavy reader use should be bound in this manner. It is strongly preferred by all libraries and book reviewers, and will almost always warrant the extra price that must be charged.

You will find that most hardback books are priced by their publishers from $8 to $16 more than their paperback counterparts. The variation depends largely on the quantity being produced and the pricing formula used.

Plastic element and spiral wire binding can be used for any reasonable page count and, in quantities of less than 250 books, can be relatively economical. This method is especially appropriate for books that need to lie flat when opened, such as cookbooks. There is also the advantage of being able to include separate tabbed dividers, which are very costly, or impossible, when used with other binding methods. Being, usually, a hand production operation, unit costs do not drop substantially in larger quantities.

The multi-ring plastic elements used are available in a wide range of standard colors and, at additional cost, special colors. Logos, titles, and other information can be silk-screened onto the elements at additional cost, or they can be left blank. In larger sizes (1¼″ and above) the elements are available with a locking device at the ends which keeps the element from springing too far open while being used. This is an excellent safety device and should be specified.

Obtaining the right-size element is important, and can be a little tricky. While tables are available that indicate the proper number of sheets for each size, they are not always reliable. An element's proper capacity will depend not only on the number of sheets, but also on paper weight, finish, and coating. The safest procedure is to have a dummy book made up and bound in the two nearest element sizes. This way you can be sure of what you are getting in advance.

If an element is too small, the pages will not turn easily and will have an increased tendency to tear out. If the element is too large, the spine takes up an excessive amount of space and the book can look awkward.

Be sure to check the punching margin to be allowed for the inside sheets. This can be varied when sheets are punched. When punched too close to the paper's edge, the sheets will tear out too easily. When punched too far in, pages will hit each other as they are turned and the punching may even cut into some of the text.

Probably the single greatest disadvantage of plastic element binding is the tear-out problem. After extended use sheets will tend to tear loose from the elements. Ideally, such books should be printed on at least an 80 lb. paper to reduce tear out and deterioration. However, since this increases paper cost and book thickness substantially, it is seldom done. In no case should paper of less than 60 lb. be used.

Chapter 5

Marketing Your Book

When a manuscript becomes a book, and is offered for sale for money, it also becomes a 'product' and is governed by the rules of the marketplace: supply and demand, needs and wants, economic value. It may be a most blessed event in the eyes of its author and his family, but it is something very different to the public being asked to buy it.

When the sales department for the Widget Manufacturing Company is asked to market a newly developed product, it will demand certain facts:

- What are the special advantages claimed for the new product?
- What are its weaknesses and limitations?
- What competitive products are already on the market?
- How are they selling? How firmly are they established?
- What are *their* special strengths, their limitations?
- How does the new product compare—in price, quality, size, appearance, buyer appeal?
- What about the market—is it saturated or wide open?

- Where is it? What is it? Who is it?
- Can it be reached, economically, with existing distribution facilities? If not, what methods will be required?
- What kind of an individual will be attracted to the product?
- What are his buying habits, his psychological profile?
- Considering all available data, *can* the product be sold, at the necessary price, at a reasonable profit?

If Widget's management is competent, it will have researched these questions while the product was still in its pilot stage—long before the company invested in its actual manufacture. Any other approach would be economically indefensible.

New books face many of the same problems and the same kinds of questions. The answers must be developed by someone, at some time prior to commitment for production.

Defining Your Market

While an author does not usually have a large capital investment in his manuscript, he does have many, many hours of valuable time, which is about the same thing. If he plans to self-publish his book, he has the additional economic concerns of any other publisher. Whatever publishing route may be taken, he certainly doesn't want to waste his time *or* his money.

The best approach is to research the market yourself, *before* you begin your manuscript.

The kind of market research required depends a good deal on whether you're writing fiction or nonfiction.

Most fiction writers build their reputations around the type of fiction that fits their personal interests and backgrounds, and then stay with that field—a mystery writer usually specializes in mysteries; a science-fiction writer in science-fiction, etc. Therefore, even if the reader markets change—as they do with gothics, for example—being 'hot' one year while westerns may be the fad the next—the fiction writer will not usually switch from his basic area of specialization merely to follow the trends.

What he will do—or should do—is to keep up with all books being published in his special area to avoid coincidental repetitions. For example, if he has been considering a mainstream novel with a plot built around the Chesapeake Bay area, and a best-seller by Michener has just been announced to the market, he may want to reconsider. He will certainly want to avoid story lines that are already overused and becoming trite.

The problem for the nonfiction writer is somewhat different. There is, sometimes, only so much that can be written, at a single point in time, about certain nonfiction subjects. If all that can be written has been written and published, is up-to-date, is by a recognized authority in the field, and is firmly established as a standard, then there is, obviously, a problem. Assuming this combination of facts, why should any publisher gamble his money on a new book on that subject? Why should bookstores want to stock it? The need has been satisfied, and when there is no need or want there is no market.

Fortunately, this is rarely the situation, and for very good reasons. It would require a tome of many thousands of pages to comprehensively cover any single subject, and the price would necessarily be high. Worst of all, no one—except researchers and scholars—would be likely to buy it. Few readers seek totally comprehensive coverage on any subject. What they do want is specific answers to specific questions or problems which currently hold their interests. They want the material to be entertainingly written, relatively easy to understand, pertinent, slanted to their individual perspectives, and they usually prefer it in 200 pages or less, at a price that doesn't represent a major investment.

Many nonfiction authors select a single, popular subject area in which they have knowledge and experience. They may write one and sometimes two books each year, gradually developing both a reputation and a loyal reader following, with each book written on a different aspect and from a different perspective on essentially the same subject area. In ten years or so they may have a dozen or more books in print. While no single book will likely make them wealthy, together the rewards can become substantial.

Such an approach is especially appropriate in the popular how-to areas. With minor periodic updatings such books can go on forever.

An author by the name of Jack Kramer, who specializes in plant and garden books, exemplifies this approach. His current books in print include:

Indoor Beauty with Vines	Walker
Begonias As House Plants	Van Nos Reinhold
The Suburban Farmer's Handbook	Doubleday
Basket Bounty	Scribner
Your Trellis Garden	Cornerstone
The Underground Gardener	Crowell
How to Feed Your Family on Five Feet of Ground	Pocketbooks
The Free Earth Guide to Gardening	Pinnacle
Natural Gardens	Scribner
Natural Way to Pest-Free Gardening	Scribner
Your First Garden	Scribner
The Indoor Gardener's How-to-Build-it Book	Simon & Schuster
Easy Plants for Difficult Places	Walker
Greenhouse Gardening Made Easy	Bantam
Your Homemade Greenhouse— How To Build It	Cornerstone
Your Window Greenhouse	Crowell
Garden Rooms and Greenhouses	Harper & Row
Flowering Plants Month by Month	Cornerstone
How to Use Houseplants Indoors for Beauty & Decoration	Doubleday
Indoor Trees	Hawthorn
A Seasonal Guide to Gardening Indoors	Hawthorn & Mifflin
One Thousand Beautiful Houseplants & How to Grow Them	Morrow
The Indoor Gardener's First Aid Book	Simon & Schuster
Plants That Grow on Air	Simon & Schuster

Bromeliads—Colorful House Plants	Van Nos Reinhold
Gardens Without Soil	Scribner
America's Outdoor Garden Build-it Book	Scribner
Miniature Plants Indoors and Out	Scribner
Orchids: Flowers of Romance & Mystery	Abrams
Orchids For Your Home	Cornerstone
Growing Orchids at Your Window	Hawthorn
Planters: Make Your Own Containers for Indoor and Outdoor Plants	Ballentine
Plants Under Lights	Simon & Schuster
Bottle Gardens	Contemp
Gardens Under Glass	Simon & Schuster
Beyond the Houseplant	Ballentine
Growing Garden Flowers Indoors	Dutton

Thirty-seven titles on what is essentially one area of expertise, and all in an area of interest that Mr. Kramer undoubtedly loves. (We may also assume that the economics of such an achievement would be equally attractive. Thirty-seven titles could easily compute to an annual royalty income of over $90,000.)

Most readers don't want to know *everything* about plants and gardens. They do want to know, at different times, how to grow orchids, how to build an indoor greenhouse, etc. Bowker's *Subject Guide To Books In Print* lists more than 60,000 different subject headings, of which 'Gardening' is only one. The number of special interest sub-areas about which one might write is staggering.

But even when books are apparently addressed to exactly the same subject or sub-subject area—as suggested by their titles—that is usually insufficient reason to abandon that subject as a possibility.

Most successful writers focus their books, consciously or unconsciously, toward a single, clearly identifiable reader. They visualize him in their minds—how he looks, where he lives, his economic, social, and educational status, his special likes, dislikes, wants and needs. They then 'talk' to that reader, as though no other existed. Of course, no writer or publisher can admit to such a restricted audience—it would reduce sales to that huge reader group that doesn't fit the profile. While every author obviously attempts to broaden the scope and usefulness of his material beyond the restricted needs of this special reader, the focus is there, however unrecognized by other readers.

This means, therefore, that many books can be written and successfully marketed on identical subjects, when they are approached from new and fresh perspectives and focused toward different readers, interests, and needs.

What other books are presently available on the subject area you have selected? *Know your competition!*

Your first step in researching other books that are currently available on your subject might be to study the card catalog of your local public library. However, this will only provide information about those books carried by that library, and will likely be inadequate for your needs.

The best source, for nonfiction books, is *Subject Guide To Books In Print*, published by R. R. Bowker Company and available through most libraries and some bookstores. All books are listed by subject, and by author. The title, publisher, binding, list price, and much more are given on all books listed. But be careful. Books are listed under many different subject headings, and often in ways that may differ from your usual way of thinking. While extensive cross-referencing is provided, it is frequently inadequate. So take some time to thumb through all parts of this multi-volume publication. To be as current as possible, also request a copy of *Subject Guide To Forthcoming Books In Print* and the *Books In Print Supplement*, and check them the same way.

After completing your search, copy the listings of the titles you have located (most libraries offer such copying services) and review your list. You will probably find one or two authors with several books listed, which suggests that they may be specializing in the area. Ask the librarian for *Books In Print—By Authors* and copy the lists of books currently in print by these authors.

You should now have a reasonably complete list of all books that are currently available in your special area of interest. Since it will probably be impossible to either locate or read all of the books involved, you may need to restrict your efforts to those titles that appear to be in direct competition with your own book. Some will be available through your library. If they aren't carried by your library, they may be available through the Inter-library Loan System, if your library is a member.

You may also want to check other libraries in your area, such as college, special, and private libraries. You will find them listed in the *American Library Directory*, also published by Bowker and available through most libraries.

Your next stop should be the major bookstores in your area. Since bookstore owners try to stock only those books that sell regularly, you can reasonably assume that any title stocked by two or more competing stores is probably selling. The reverse is less true, however. The fact that a title is not stocked does not necessarily mean it is not selling well in other cities. Most bookstore owners feel that they do not need, and cannot afford, to tie up the space and capital to stock several competing titles on a single restricted subject, so they may select one or the other, without prejudice to the title omitted.

Meet the bookstore owner. Explain your project. Ask him (or her) to share his experience. Which books, within your subject area, sell best? Which sell worst? Why? What special needs or 'holes' does he see in the area that may offer special opportunities? Do hardbacks or paperbacks sell best? Which publishers does he recommend for the subject involved? What other avenues of investigation would he suggest?

You will also find, in many areas, a local Bookstore Owners Association. If so, be sure to join it, support it, attend its meetings, and meet its members. You will find them to be a splendid group of people.

Bookstore owners must cope with the realities of the marketplace every day. They either learn—quickly—what sells and what doesn't, or they go broke! The idealistic inclinations about the 'world of books' they may have once held have long since been merged with the inexorable pressures of basic economics. Consequently, they can be a new author's most reliable advisor.

There are, of course, many other excellent sources of marketing information. Every serious writer should subscribe to *Publisher's Weekly*, published by R. R. Bowker Company, and *Writer's Digest. The Encyclopedia of Associations*, published by Gale Research Company, provides information access to thousands of organizations and associations representing every conceivable area or interest. *Writer's Research Handbook: The Bible for Freelance Writers*, published by Barnes and Noble Books, and *Finding Facts Fast—How to Find Out What You Want to Know Immediately,* published by William Morrow & Co., provide a wealth of source information that can be invaluable to every writer.

However you accomplish it—and if you are imaginative and determined you will find hundreds of ways—you need to develop an in-depth understanding of what is presently available on your subject area, along with an honest, realistic evaluation of specifically why the material you intend to offer is better, more up-to-date, more entertaining, or of greater value to the readers who will be asked to buy it. If you cannot convince yourself that this is true, you will probably have a hard time convincing others.

Know your subject. Know your reader. Know your competition. Know that you have a product that is needed. Once you have established such a solid foundation, the rest is relatively easy.

Selling Your Book

After many months of concentrated effort, you have finished your manuscript. Every 'i' is dotted; every 't' is crossed. If you are a self-publisher, your manuscript is in the capable hands of your book printer. You are through; you have finally done it!

Well, brace yourself. The fun has just begun. Even if you have written a second *Gone With The Wind*, don't expect the world of book buyers to come knocking on your door—not in today's publicity-oriented society. They just won't do it.

Nor should you think that you would be off the hook if your book had been published by a giant among trade publishers. That isn't the way it works. They would require your services to help promote your book. If your book was planned to be a real seller, you would be facing interviews, talk shows, autograph parties—the list goes on.

There is simply no alternative. If you are a shy, modest, retiring individual who avoids the limelight like the plague, now is the time for your personal metamorphosis; for coming out of your shell.

The author is the single most influencing factor in the sale of a book. If you are excited and exciting, enthusiastic, outgoing, indomitable, friendly, and energetic (or can at least present such an image), you've already won half the battle.

To those unacquainted with the marketing profession (promotion, publicity, advertising, selling, and distribution) the process sometimes seems like a mysterious mixture of pressure and persuasion, with a little 'con' thrown in for good measure. Because of this, some writers feel uncomfortable with the entire process.

In truth, however, at least 75 percent of the marketing process is simply effective communication, and most of that is pursued in a relatively definable manner. Marketing can be described as the simple act of letting potential buyers know that a product exists, describing it factually, and persuasively explaining its benefits. Obviously the communication required should be handled in a friendly, courteous, and helpful manner that leaves those involved in a receptive frame of mind. But they certainly do not need to be misled.

This all presupposes, of course, that the product (in this case, your book) has merit. If it doesn't, it shouldn't have been published in the first place, and all of the advertising and promotion in the world will not turn it into a success. But if it does—and you believe that it does—it surely deserves a fair hearing.

Organize your plan of attack and establish a budget.

Except for the blockbusters by big-name authors, most trade publishers set their promotion and advertising budgets at amounts equal to about 10 percent of the list price value of a book's first printing. If you are printing 5,000 copies of a book with a list price of $12 this means a budget of $6,000. That's not a great deal of money, so you must be careful. With today's high advertising rates you can spend a small fortune, and still end up with nothing to show for it. The trick is to get the maximum possible results from every single dollar you spend. And the way to do that is to take full advantage of every free or almost-free publicity service that is available to you. Fortunately, there are many such services available within the book industry.

A Marketing Program

The following step-by-step marketing program fully utilizes those services. It also tells you the best time to do what. It is, of course, only one approach and may be varied in any way you feel is best. But one thing is certain: if you follow all the steps outlined—and you have a book that truly fills a need in a credible way—*you will sell books!*

Step 1. First, decide on and set a formal publication date. It should be about six months in the future, and well after (six to eight weeks) the date your books are scheduled for delivery from your book printer. There is a common misconception that these two dates must be the same, but that isn't true. One of the most important referencing publications, *Forthcoming Books In Print*, requires six months lead time for new listings. Also, most reviewers will not consider a book unless it is submitted to them well in advance of the announced publication date. This leeway is also important to allow time to obtain endorsements, advance reader comments, and reviews, all of which can be used in later publicity. *Many books have already been through two or more printings by the time the formal publication date is reached.*

Step 2. Have your book listed in *Forthcoming Books In Print*. To do this, you must first obtain, fill out, and return an 'Advance Book Information Form.' Address your request to ABI Department, R. R. Bowker Company, 245 W. 17th St.,

New York, NY 10011. This form should be filed six months prior to your publication date. This publication is recognized by the entire book industry, especially libraries and bookstores. Listings are free.

Step 3. Obtain a copy of *Literary Market Place*. This is the single most authoritative marketing guide to the book industry available. It includes, among many other things, lists of book reviewers, editors, publishers, book clubs, magazines and newspapers, radio and television networks, news services, book trade events, associations, and mailing list suppliers.

This is an annual publication which currently sells for $90.25 and may be ordered from R. R. Bowker Company. While expensive, it should be in the personal library of every serious author/publisher. If you are dealing with a book specialist, he will probably let you use his copy. Copies are also available at most public libraries. LMP is truly an extraordinary reference tool.

Write to several of the mailing list suppliers listed in *Literary Market Place* requesting a free copy of their general mailing lists catalog. These catalogs will not only tell you about the thousands of special mailing lists that are available, the size of each market, and the cost of the lists involved, but they will also open your eyes to new markets which you may not have known of or thought about before. Spend some time reviewing these catalogs, page by page. It will be time well spent. You will probably end up with a whole new world of marketing possibilities for your book.

Step 4. Develop a prepublication 'News Release' on your book. The masthead should be set in printer's type with the announcement itself set in typewriter type.

Write your news release in a direct, no-nonsense, newspaper style with the most important information in the first paragraph so that it can stand alone if necessary. Include the title and subtitle of the book, the list price, a brief synopsis of the contents, the kind of binding to be used, information about yourself as author (especially your qualifications for writing on the subject covered), the name of your publishing company, the address to which orders can be sent, and your formal publication date.

Your picture, or a picture of your book, can be included as part of the news release. A glossy 8″ x 10″ black-and-white photograph should be attached, if possible. The dust jacket can be included also, if it has been printed.

A prepublication news release can serve double duty by including a tear-off order form at the bottom. For book reviewers, this form can be designed as a request for a review copy of the book itself. A second tear-off form can be designed for other recipients for use as an advance, prepublication order form (at a special prepublication price, if you desire). While this technique requires the printing of two separate news releases, one for each tear-off form, it is well worth the small additional cost.

Step 5. As soon as possible, but never less than eight weeks before your publication date, announce your book to the four main prepublication reviewing media: *Publisher's Weekly*, 249 W. 17th St. New York, NY 10011; *Library Journal,* 249 W. 17th St. New York, NY 10011; *Kirkus Reviews* 200 Park Avenue, New York, NY 10003; and *Forecast,* published by the Baker and Taylor Companies, Box 6920, 652 E. Main St., Bridgewater, NJ 08807-0920.

A brief cover letter, offering your book for review, should be accompanied by your news release and galley, or page proofs, of the book itself. (Proofs can be provided by your book printer at additional cost.) If a news release has not been prepared, all pertinent information about your book should be provided in the letter itself. If your book is to be hardbound this fact should be stressed. Be sure to ask that the address from which books may be ordered be included in the review.

Step 6. Next, send your prepublication news release to a select list of other reviewers. A national list can be developed from *Literary Market Place.* In addition, however, regional newspapers, radio and television stations, and magazines should be included. If your book is of potential interest to special interest groups you should send news releases to national magazines that cater to those groups. You will find several hundred such magazines listed, by subject, in *Writer's Market.*

Don't forget the civic, social, educational, professional, fraternal, and religious organizations in your area. If your book includes references to local families—such as those often included in books on regional history—be sure to let them know about it.

Step 7. Finally, your book is printed and delivered—and you can now go to work in earnest! The first requirement, which should be handled promptly, is to make your formal copyright application. (See 'Copyrighting Your Book' in Chapter 3.) Include two copies of the actual book and a check for $10. Mail, in one package, to the Register of Copyrights, Library of Congress, Washington, D.C. 20559.

Step 8. If you have received a Library of Congress number, send one copy of your book to Library of Congress, C.I.P. Office, Washington, D.C. 20540.

Step 9. Send one copy of your book, accompanied by an 'Information Sheet,' to each of the indexing, referencing and reviewing publications serving the book industry. They include: the 'Weekly Record' of *Publisher's Weekly,* 249 W. 17th St., New York, NY 10011; *Library Journal,* 249 W. 17th St., New York, NY 10011; *Cumulative Book Index,* a monthly publication of H. W. Wilson Co., 950 University Avenue, Bronx, NY 10452; and *Books in Print, Subject Guide to Books in Print,* and *Publishers Trade List Annual,* all published by R. R. Bowker Co., 245 W. 17th St., New York, NY 10011. (Write R. R. Bowker Co. for information and instructions prior to sending actual book.)

While information requirements vary between these companies, an Information Sheet which includes the following will satisfy all of them: title and subtitle, name of the author, year of publication, size of book, number of pages, number of illustrations, kind of binding, retail price, subject and table of contents, name and address from which book can be ordered, ISBN number, Library of Congress number.

Step 10. Send a complimentary copy of your book,

accompanied by your news release and information sheet, to a select list of the larger national book jobbers as well as any regional jobbers that serve your trade area. Three large national jobbers are: Academic Library Services, Baker & Taylor Co., Box 6920, 652 E. Main St., Bridgewater, NJ 08807-0920; American Library Association, 50 East Huron Street, Chicago, IL 60611 and Bro-Dart Books, Inc., 500 Arch St., Williamsport, PA 17705. (See *Literary Market Place* for additional listings.)

Step 11. Now that your book is in print you should follow up on any request for review copies you may have received from your prepublication news releases. A copy of your book, with a letter reminding them of their earlier requests, should be sent to each reviewer. You should also review your original list and send a copy of your book to those with real potential even though they may not have specifically requested it.

Copies of your book must be sent to reviewers six to eight weeks prior to your announced publication date. Many reviewers will not accept books for review after the publication date.

If you did not send out prepublication news releases be sure to develop one now to include with your review copy. Remember that many publications, especially the smaller newspapers and magazines, have small staffs and will often pick up all or part of a news release exactly as it is written. So write your release exactly the way you want potential book buyers to read it. Be sure to tell about yourself, with emphasis on your special qualifications for writing on the subject covered by your book. If you have already received some good reviews, enclose copies. They lend credibility.

Step 12. If your book is on a subject of interest to special groups, there will almost always be one or many magazines that are focused toward such groups. *Writer's Market* describes many such magazines. The *Ayer Directory of Publications*, available from your book specialist or your library, lists and describes virtually every magazine and newspaper published in the U.S. and Canada. Listings are also available from *Literary Market Place*.

While you may not want to send review copies of your book to many such magazines, you should at least send copies to a few of the leaders in the areas involved. News releases should be sent to the rest.

Step 13. Feature stories about books and their authors are regularly included in all newspapers and Sunday supplements. If you or your book are really interesting, if your subject is new, innovative, highly topical, or controversial, the odds are excellent that it could be turned into a feature story. Scan as many issues of as many newspapers—including the national tabloids—as you can get your hands on. Check the by-lines, and then write or call the reporters named to inquire about the possibilities of such a feature story about your book. Meet him (or her) in person, if possible. Be enthusiastic; be excited and energetic. Help him to understand and believe in you and your book, as you do.

Once one feature story has been run it can be used as a stimulus for more such stories. You will be amazed at how the process can snowball.

Step 14. You are now ready for the television and radio talk shows. Talk shows are becoming increasingly popular at both the local and national level. As they expand in time allotments, their appetites for new materials and new faces become increasingly voracious. They need a continuing supply of new guests with new ideas to offer, just as much as you need the exposure which they can provide for you and your book. It has been stated by one New York literary agent that a thirty second exposure on a national talk show will sell more books than a full page ad in the New York *Times.* Even this is probably an understatement. Few authors can afford an expenditure for advertising that could equal the impact that a successful talk show campaign can provide free. Such exposures can also do wonders in establishing an author's reputation not only as a writer, but as an expert and a personality.

Surprisingly, local talk shows are not nearly as difficult to set up as is usually thought. But invitations do depend a great deal on the subject covered by the book. Most local talk show formats are geared toward upbeat, topical subjects, and their producers will usually reject any subject that they consider to be 'yesterday's news' or that will leave their audiences depressed.

The key to talk show acceptance is energy, determination, and a sense of humor. It is often hard to reach the person in control, the one who can say 'yes' or 'no.' For this reason letters are not often too successful. Probably the most effective method is to dig—by telephone—until you finally reach the right person. Describe your book, your special approach to your subject, and your own background. You should especially stress your credentials for writing the book. Ask for an appointment to discuss your request. Then follow up your conversation with a letter directed to that person.

It is an excellent idea to record or videotape your first few talk shows. Most stations have the facilities required, and the cost is reasonable. The copies can then be used as 'promos' to interest other talk show hosts, especially those located at the national level, as well as those in other major cities.

Don't shy away from the national talk shows. While they are naturally more selective, and they will only be interested in subjects that have national appeal, they can be 'cracked.' And they can mean a gold mine in book sales, not to mention their influence on subsidiary sales.

Step 15. Many self-publishers have professional status or recognizable expertise in their special field of interest. This is usually the reason they wrote their book in the first place. Most such writers are energetic, enthusiastic, and outgoing— 'leaders' in every sense of the word.

Such individuals are ideal candidates for speaking engagements. Having written a book makes them doubly attractive.

Service clubs, civic clubs, hobby clubs, library associations, etc., are constantly in need of guest speakers. By simply letting them know that you are available you will probably have more requests than you can handle. Speaking engagements, like talk shows, sell books and build reputations. Use them!

Step 16. Meet your area booksellers and librarians. They are, almost without exception, splendid people. They love books, and they enjoy helping serious new authors. They can also be a source of invaluable counsel and advice which is available nowhere else.

Many libraries have supporting associations which meet regularly and most bookstore owners belong to a regional association of booksellers which also holds regular meetings. Invitations to either will give you a chance to make wonderful friends and gain supporters for your book. Bookstore owners may be interested in setting up autograph parties at their stores, which can be valuable.

Step 17. Don't forget those retailers that are outside of the traditional book industry. Department stores and drug stores usually have book departments—often very large and successful ones. Lumber yards, home improvement stores, health stores, garden nurseries, hobby shops, sporting goods stores, and children's stores all sell books, often in astonishing quantities. Contact them.

Step 18. Book wholesalers and jobbers handle hundreds of thousands of titles each year. Some, like Baker and Taylor or Ingram Books, are very large, with many distribution centers; others operate mainly on a regional basis. Some have outside salesmen calling on bookstores; most rely on telephone orders and periodic mailings of stock lists and other promotional announcements.

While discounts vary depending on the quantity of books ordered, most wholesalers work on 50 to 60 percent of list price, of which 20 to 45 percent is passed on the retailer.

Many wholesalers see their function as efficient warehousers, relieving publishers of the burden of small unit orders and booksellers of having to take up both space and money on slow turning books. The average shipping time for single book orders from national publishers is about four to six weeks; booksellers can special order books from wholesalers and receive titles, when they are in stock, in seven to ten days—and at about the same discount.

The problem with wholesalers is that they can usually only afford to warehouse established titles that will turn on a regular basis, which is not the case with all books on all subjects. Most of the smaller wholesalers specialize in clearly definable subject areas or book categories. Massmarket paperbacks are traditionally distributed by magazine jobbers as an outgrowth of their distribution of magazines and their established relationships with drug stores, grocery stores and similar retail outlets.

Books are also becoming popular staples for other wholesalers not commonly associated with the industry. Stationery distributors regularly stock dictionaries and secretarial reference books. Health food distributors carry a wide range of books dealing with nutrition and natural foods, including cookbooks and diet books. Lumber and hardware distributors often carry lines of home, garden, and how-to books. Toy store wholesalers carry juvenile books, picture books, game books, and puzzle books. The list and possibilities are almost endless. A list of national book wholesalers can be found in *Literary Market Place*.

Step 19. The chain bookstores can turn your book into an overnight success story, if they choose to do so. There are not many, but they can mean really big sales. If your book has national sales appeal, contact them. Call on them in person, if you can arrange an advance appointment. The money invested in the trip can be repaid many times over, and very quickly.

You will find a listing of chain bookstores, with the names of their main-office buyers, in *American Book Trade Directory*, published by R. R. Bowker Co. Copies of this directory may be available at your local library or in the library of your book specialist. Two of the larger ones are:

Doubleday Book Shops
666 Fifth Avenue, New York, NY 10103

Dayton-Hudson (Pickwick & B. Dalton)
4137 Timberlane Dr., Allison Park, PA 15101

Step 20. Don't forget the libraries. It is reported that 75 percent of the income on children's books is from institutions, mainly schools and libraries. They also buy large quantities of other kinds of books. Best of all they pay dependably and do not usually require large discounts.

There are about 72,000 libraries in this country alone. The public libraries number 9,000; there are over 3,000 college libraries, 17,000 public high school libraries, and 43,000 elementary school libraries. There are also many special libraries—and they all buy books.

Purchases of new books are usually handled by the Acquisitions Director. Contact the libraries in your area in person. National mailing lists are available from R. R. Bowker Company and all mailing list suppliers. (See Step 22.)

Step 21. Conventions and exhibits may be tiring, but they provide an excellent way to get exposure for your books. If your subject concerns a special industry or field, find out where their conventions are to be held. A listing of most national associations is given in the *Encyclopedia of Associations*, published by Gale Research Company and available at your library.

Sponsors of major book exhibits include:

The American Booksellers Association
137 W. 25th St., New York, NY 10001

The American Library Association
50 East Huron St., Chicago, IL 60611

The National Association of College Stores
528 East Lorain St., Oberlin, OH 44074

The Christian Booksellers Association
2620 Venetucci Blvd.
Colorado Springs, CO 80901

Services are also available which display books for several publishers on a per book fee basis. Since you do not have to personally attend the exhibits it becomes very economical. Companies offering such services include:

American Bookdealers Exchange
Box 2525, La Mesa, CA 92041

BMI Educational Services
Hay Press Rd., Dayton, NJ 08810

The Conference Book Service, Inc.
80 S. Early St., Alexandria, VA 22304

The New England Mobile Book Fair, Inc.
Box 340, 82-84 Needham St.
Newton Highlands, MA 02161

Step 22. Twenty-five percent of all book purchases originate from mail-order promotion. If your book should be directed to special interest markets which are scattered over a wide geographic area, this can be the most effective—and sometimes the only—way to reach them. Check the mailing list catalogs discussed in Step 3 to select the most appropriate markets and the costs involved.

But remember this: marketing by mail is not a hit-or-miss game for amateurs; it is both an art and a science that requires skill and experience. A simple home-made flier just won't do.

Mail advertising, especially at today's postal rates, is expensive. It can easily amount to 35 to 50 percent of the list price value of your sales. It can also involve a considerable amount of book returns, depending on the kind of offer you make in your promotion.

The percent of orders received from mail advertising promotion is small, averaging about 2 percent or less. If you have a really special book that fills a real and recognized need, or a book on a 'hot' subject, you may be able to achieve order returns of up to 5 percent. Anything higher is a miracle!

It is also a fact of life that low dollar products (like paperback books) are just not economically feasible for mail-order sale. The unit price must be relatively high and the gross profit margin must be substantial—at least 60 to 80 percent—to beat the odds.

Don't try to do-it-yourself! Get help from a mail order specialist with a proven track record, if possible. He can, and usually will, tell you in advance whether your efforts will pay off or not. If he believes they will, he can design and produce a mailing piece that gives the best possible chance for success.

Co-op mailing services are also available. Most specialize in certain selected market areas, such as the bookstore and library markets. They put out mailings on a regular basis, each of which includes fliers from several different publishers. In this way costs for each advertiser are substantially reduced from what they would be otherwise if each were mailed individually.

As previously stated, a list of mailing list suppliers is given in *Literary Market Place.*

You do not have to rent entire mailing lists. All are computer-coded by zip codes and many are coded in a wide range of other ways. Check the specific selections available. They will not only help you test your mailing on a smaller scale but can also substantially improve your odds for success.

Step 23. Many self-publishers have had success using the classified sections of national magazines. The costs of small ads are relatively low, and returns can be good for certain kinds of books—especially if the title explains the subject.

The biggest problem is with the cheats and frauds who are ruining this approach. They advertise inviting titles at high prices and then send out a sloppy, worthless, mimeographed, typewritten handful of sheets stapled together. If such deceptions are allowed to continue this potentially excellent medium will soon be destroyed. The magazine publishers can stop it, if they will, by demanding advance samples of the books being offered for sale. In spite of its problems it is still a medium worth considering.

Step 24. We come at last to that medium which is usually first in the minds of most new authors: space advertising. Certainly it requires minimum effort—you pay your money, sit back, and wait.

Unfortunately, it can also be economically disastrous, especially for the low-budget, one-book author. Every reliable, experienced advertising agency will quickly tell you that space ads must be big enough and consistent enough to do the job intended or they are worthless. The problem is that such advertising is very expensive, especially in terms of cost per thousand readers when it must be limited to local markets. A full page ad in a large metropolitan newspaper will cost many thousands of dollars; even small ads will eat up a restricted advertising budget in short order. It is almost statistically impossible for any single-book publisher to economically justify such expenditures. So, it should be approached very cautiously.

Yet, to prove that there is an exception to every rule, I have one client who regularly runs full-page ads, at exhorbitant costs, in such national publications as *Mother Earth News* and the *National Enquirer*—and they apparently pay off.

You will notice that most of the above marketing suggestions are either free or almost free. This is the real key to selling books at a profit. In the long run *it is not really how many books you sell, but whether you end up in the black.* Even when profits are not your primary goal and motivation, there are still definite limits as to how much you can afford to lose. *Books can be sold by self-publishers, at a profit.* It is happening every day, and you can do it too. But it requires planning, work, and determination (plus a book that fills a real need). How much of this work you will choose to do on your own is up to you and your budget. Many marketing organizations are available to help in any phase where they may be needed. If you are working with a full-service book specialist, he will be able to provide assistance in many areas.

Pricing Your Book

New author/publishers have a tendency to price their books as low as possible. They operate on the theory that lower prices will mean higher sales, which in turn will result in more profit, eventually. Some also feel, subconsciously perhaps, that it is unethical to price anything—books included—at more than twice the direct costs involved. A few are so uncertain about the market acceptance for their book that they are afraid that a high price will destroy all possibilities for significant sales.

Such theories are not only incorrect, but *they are a certain road to publishing bankruptcy.* Unless you have a potential best-seller on your hands, you will need every nickel that the market will bear to pay all the costs and expenses involved and to make a profit.

The fact is that *price has little to do with book sales*, provided that established traditions and psychological barriers are not upset. There is no valid evidence to prove that pricing a hardback book $1 higher or $1 lower will affect sales one iota. If the book is needed or wanted, attractive, professionally written and manufactured, and properly promoted, stocked and displayed, it will sell at any reasonable price. If not, it won't.

On the other hand, well-established traditions cannot be flaunted. Book buyers know and understand the 'normal' price range for mass-market paperbacks. They also know the price range for quality paperbacks. Regardless of the author's reputation, the extent of the research involved, or the number of pages, they somehow feel cheated when they are asked to pay substantially more than current norms.

To a lesser degree similar pricing restrictions apply to hardback books. Though acceptable price levels gradually change with time and inflation, readers have a value barometer within their minds for every hardback book they may thumb through. When the price exceeds that level, regardless of the book's real value, they tend to back off. Not so much because of the absolutes involved, but because of what they perceive to be a disbalance of relationships.

While few books can be successfully priced beyond these subjective barriers, they can and must be priced as close to them as possible. The high discounts required by wholesalers and retail booksellers, the enormous cost of promotion and advertising, and the high risk and investment of both time and money all demand a substantial margin between list price and direct manufacturing cost. Any other policy is economic suicide.

Though it varies by kind of book, market, and avenue of sale, the list price of books is traditionally established by book publishers throughout the industry at levels that average six to eight times reprint direct costs, including royalties. So if the unit cost of a book is $1.50, for example, it should sell for from $9 to $12. (Or, accepting the psychology of the marketplace, from $8.95 to $11.95.) The question is, how do you compute unit cost, in advance, when you don't know, with any degree of certainty, how many books will eventually be sold or how many reprintings will be called for.

It is impossible to compute a realistic unit cost without assuming a total quantity to be printed. This quantity is usually considered to be the quantity to be printed during the first year. Yet, it is rarely more than an educated guess, since no one can say with certainty what number of books will be sold. The effect of this guess on list price is significant. If the first printing is for 5,000 copies, the unit cost may compute to $2.50 per book; if the first printing is for 10,000 copies, the unit cost may be only $1.50 per book.

Savings involved in subsequent printings are even more significant. The first printing must bear the full cost of editing, art work, typesetting, paging, and negatives—all of which constitute a significant portion of the total. A book with a first printing unit cost of $2.00 may drop to as little as $1.00 when the book is reprinted immediately, even in the same quantity. If the reprint quantity is larger, unit costs will drop even more.

Frankly, there is no statistically valid answer. In the final analysis it all comes down to the extent of one's optimism. Since almost any unit cost can be substantiated, what should be done?

It is my conviction that unit costs, and hence list prices, should be computed on the basis of a full year's anticipated production schedule, recognizing that changes may be required. This schedule should anticipate the number of reprints, and quantities for each, for the entire year. If the total cost of such a schedule, which can be quoted by your book printer, is $22,000 for a total production of, say, 20,000 books, your unit cost would be $1.10 per book. Using a 8:1 ratio as a guide, this would place the list price as $8.80. But if evidence can be found which shows that comparable size and quality books are successfully selling for, say, $9.95, the lower figure should be ignored and the higher one used. *One thing is certain: that extra margin will be needed before all is done.*

Discounts

If books are to be sold by mail, they should be priced as high as possible. The cost of mail order selling is usually at least as high as the discounts required by jobbers and retailers and often higher.

Books sold through trade jobbers and booksellers will have to be discounted to pay for the services rendered by those firms. There are about as many discount arrangements as there are publishers, and almost any schedule can be defended, or damned, depending on one's perspective.

The simplest method, which is probably as good as any, is to offer a single discount schedule for wholesalers and retailers alike, based on the number of books ordered.

5-25 books	40 percent
25-49 books	43 percent
50-99 books	46 percent
100 books & over	50 percent

If a wholesaler is doing his job he will be able to order and stock at least 100 copies of a book and will receive the full 50 percent discount. If a bookseller is doing *his* job he will stock at least 5 copies, giving him 40 percent. This gives the wholesaler a 10 point spread which equals a 20 percent mark-up on his cost. It also allows the bookseller not stocking the book to make 20 percent on special orders which he may place with the wholesaler.

Some jobbers, however, will probably insist that their discount must be 60 percent of list, giving them a 40 percent mark-up on their cost. The single-book publisher will especially be confronted with such pressures. The decision is one which only you can make.

Discount policies for schools and libraries are less clear and they vary widely within the industry. Since non-resale institutions often place single copy orders, the handling and processing cost is very high, with no really large orders to offset it. Also, unlike bookstores, they will reorder the same book infrequently, if at all. This means that the one-book publisher will often spend more time and money opening his charge accounts and processing his orders than the sales may be worth. This is especially true when complicated requisition and order forms are used by such customers.

Probably the most reasonable solution is to allow a 20 percent discount on orders of five books or more, but to charge full list price on all smaller orders.

Freight & Postage

It is fairly standard policy within the book industry that freight and postage are added to all invoices that involve trade discounts. Policies for list price sales vary, but postage and handling are usually added to the invoice on mail order sales.

Returns

Book return policies for bookstores are, traditionally, very liberal. Many publishers state that any book may be returned for credit within not less than three months or more than twelve months after purchase, provided the books are undamaged and in salable condition, return shipping costs are prepaid by the bookstore, the publisher has been notified in advance so that shipping instructions can be given, and a copy of the original invoice accompanies the shipment. When a copy of the original invoice is not provided, books will be credited at 50 percent of list price.

Terms of Payment

Most publishers allow bookstores a 2 percent cash discount when payment is made within ten days of invoice date; invoices are due net thereafter, and are past due in thirty days (2/10; net/30). Many bookstores, however, are traditionally slow payers, often taking sixty to ninety days to pay their bills. And, when pressed too hard, they simply stop buying from that publisher, especially if he is small and they can survive without his line of books.

The problem of small publishers getting their money on time, and for the relatively small amounts usually involved, is one that demands real diplomacy. The best solution is to develop a warm, friendly—but professional—relationship from the start. Astutely handled, a slow-paying customer can be converted into a prompt payer, and maintained as a loyal supporter at the same time.

STOP

Many publishers participate in an ordering plan called STOP (Single Title Order Plan—formerly called 'SCOP') which is sponsored by the American Booksellers Association. This plan allows booksellers to order one or more copies of single titles on a specially designed order blank, attaching an 'open amount' check to be filled in by the publisher. This is an excellent program which eliminates much of the costly paperwork involved in such small orders.

Highly recommended.

Consignment

Almost every new, small publisher, at one time or another, begins to think about consignment sales as a way to boost his volume and profits. The problem is that it *rarely works.* The necessary controls are costly and time consuming to administer, misunderstandings are almost inevitable, it rarely helps sales, and most bookstores don't want to be bothered.

Best bet: forget it.

Consistency

Whatever policies you may adopt, and they are entirely up to you, it is extremely important that you publish them in your trade literature, leave nothing to question, and follow those policies consistently. Nothing infuriates a retailer more than having to continually correspond concerning arbitrary changes or discrepancies in prices, discounts and payment terms.

Shipping, Billing & Collection

After the euphoria of first orders has finally worn off, the least exciting aspect of book publishing, for most author/publishers, is the routine requirements of order handling.

But it is, in reality, what the entire process has been all about. It is not enough to write, produce, and sell a good book. The orders which are received must be efficiently handled and converted into money, which you can then use to pay your own bills. In spite of this obvious fact, the sloppy, unprofessional handling of orders and paperwork probably creates more ill-will within the trade for small, single-book publishers than all other problems combined.

The root of the difficulty lies in its scope, or rather the lack of it. There are usually just enough orders trickling in each day to be a 'pain in the neck', but rarely enough to warrant hiring a full time office-warehouse worker to handle them. As a result many small publishers attempt to handle all orders personally or to enlist the aid of family and friends. Which, in the beginning, is fine. But finally the newness wears off, more interesting tasks beckon, and the decision is made to handle orders on a weekly basis, which soon extends to twice a month, etc., and orders and correspondence begin to stack up.

The best answer depends on how you value your time. If your time is worth money and can be more profitably spent on other activities, you should make specific arrangements, from the beginning, to have professionals handle the entire storage-shipping-billing sequence for you. While the cost per book may seem high, it will rarely be as high as your doing-it-yourself, especially if you place a realistic hourly rate on your time.

Check your suburban phone book or classified ads. You will probably find secretarial services or home typists located nearby. They are usually ideal for the special requirements involved. Or you may want to consult with a local mailing firm. Some book printers and book specialists will handle these activities for you on a routine basis. There are also national 'fulfillment' companies available, many of which are listed in *LMP*.

Whatever you decide, at least decide this: *orders and correspondence must be handled—promptly, professionally, accurately.*

There are a few printed forms you will need: invoices, shipping labels, packing lists, etc. You will also need letter-heads, envelopes, and calling cards. All of these items can be obtained through your local office supply store. They will have samples from which you can select, and attractive designs which you can adapt. All are available in small quantities at reasonable costs.

You will also need packages and cartons for shipping and mailing. For individual orders the 'Jiffy' insulated bag is the best and most economical. It is available in many sizes through your office supply dealer or, in larger quantities, from paper wholesalers. For multi-book orders you can buy knock-down corrugated boxes from local container manu-facturers or distributors.

If your marketing approach involves credit sales, you may want to set up a simple accounts receivable ledger system, using a separate page for each charge customer. When this becomes unwieldly, as it will when several hundred customers are involved, you may want to talk to one of the many computer service companies that are now available. Many specialize in accounts receivable services and can provide a complete service, which includes statements, analysis of sales, and control reports, at very reasonable rates.

You will, no doubt, want to take full advantage of all legitimate tax deductions and advantages that are available from your writing/publishing activities. The best way to insure this happy result is to maintain complete and accurate records that are totally spearated from your personal finances. You should, from the very beinning, establish a separate bank account for your business activities. Transfer a reasonable amount from your personal checking or savings account, clearly identified as your original investment. *Do not, if at all possible, switch monies back and forth.* Every item of expense or cost that relates to your writing/publishing venture should be paid through this business account, and all monies received, whether by cash or by check, must be deposited to it.

Keep clean, separate records of everything you do. In this way your tax accountant will be able to handle your tax situation in the most advantageous, legal way possible.

Chapter 6

Opportunities
for Writers

Aside from dreams of fame and fortune, *why do writers* write? Why do they subject themselves, again and again, to the agony and frustration of that blank page, demanding to be filled? Those precious pearls of insight, so compelling through the sleepless hours of night, have fled, returning once more to the depths of that creative darkness from whence they sprang, unbidden.

Most writers write because they *must*. Something deep inside, some mysterious compulsion, literally *forces* them to write. Writing, for such writers, is simply one of many natural functions which, for better or worse, must be carried out.

Others write because they have a story to tell, experiences to relate, problems and solutions to pass on, truths to be shared. They are important. They need to be communicated.

Still others write because they have an overwhelming sense of responsibility to civilization; a deep understanding of the building blocks of collected knowledge upon which mankind moves toward its destiny. In recent decades societies throughout the world have undergone traumatic experiences and disillusionments. They have learned that no one and no group have all the solutions that man requires to lift the heavy burdens that he carries. Such answers as *can* be found must come from all of us. *Every* individual has a contribution he can make, drawn from his own experiences, knowledge, skills, studies, and observations. And each of us, surely, has a responsibility to do so, when we can.

Writing As Self-Expression

The basic human need for self-expression is one of the most elemental forces compelling most writers to write.

Man is an expressionistic being. He longs to translate the reality of his inner self into tangible, observable, and handleable forms; to capture and display the fleeting wisps of his genius, insight, and understanding that swiftly and elusively scurry across the heavens of his consciousness, fading and disappearing so quickly, sometimes forever.

Each man attempts to satisfy this need in ways that have meaning to *him*, depending on his nature, talents, abilities, training, education, and opportunities. Some become carpenters, builders, contractors, or architects. Others become artists, musicians, or actors. Still others find their areas of self-expression in building a business, contesting for political office, or in courts of law.

A writer finds his own area of self-expression and personal fulfillment through *words on paper*. This, to him, is the most direct form of expression, the most precise and accurate form of communication. To him, *words are things*. But more importantly, words transcend things and thereby speak to and of that exciting and mysterious world of non-things: human emotions, ideas, judgments, intuition, creativity, imagination, hopes, and dreams.

Not that the writer is necessarily alienated from the world of physical expression. He may, in fact, be very much a part of, even a leader in, that world of action. Certainly, at his best, he allows himself—even forces himself—to be caught up in all the torment, risks, and ecstacy of that world, if only to broaden his own experiences and to more sharply hone the edge of his personal judgment and understanding. But he always returns from his forays and adventures to his central role as observer, recorder, explainer, and interpreter of the essence that he has captured and synthesized within his fertile mind.

Writing As Communication

Communication is another basic need that is essential to most humans. Few of us can survive, indefinitely, in isolation and solitude, cut off from all forms of social contact. Such isolation is an ancient and effective form of torture against those who have violated the rules of their social group.

But communication takes many forms. Some scientists believe that most of our communicating devices are non-verbal. The movement of the head, the lowering of an eyelid, the stiffening of the jaw—these and hundreds of other silent and subtle signals may transmit a message with greater force and effectiveness than words.

Yet, the most precise and enduring form of communication that man has devised is still found in the miracle of words and language. And, while verbal communication is the mode most commonly employed under the daily pressures of social intercourse, it can rarely equal, in accuracy, reflection, care, consideration, the artistry of presentation and word selection, indexing, referencing, and durability, the many advantages of its written counterpart.

How many hearts and friendships have been damaged or destroyed by an inconsiderate phrase or emotional outburst? How many seeds of bitterness and hate have been sown by a poorly chosen word which did not, in fact, accurately convey the intentions of the speaker? What is so powerful as words?

Words, and the ideas they convey, are stronger than steel and more powerful than bombs. With words, Gandhi directed the destinies of 400 million Indians. With words, Hitler constructed an organization that slaughtered 6 million Jews. With words, the founding fathers of America developed a system of freedom that altered the face of the world. And with words, Marx developed an ideology that could enslave the hearts and minds of mankind forever.

While we must communicate, each of us do so most effectively in our own special way. For some this means verbal communication, and in this mode they may be eloquent and persuasive—yet be struck dumb when forced to write.

To others the opposite is true. In public address or even private conversation they may be shy, taciturn, and desperately uncomfortable. Yet, with pen and paper a metamorphosis occurs, and a new self takes wings, often to the bewilderment of acquaintances.

There is no apparent rhyme nor reason for the many and diverse avenues which the need for communication may choose. But whatever the explanation or scientific basis, one blessed with the talent to communicate should be grateful, and develop it to the full richness that it deserves.

Writing provides such opportunities in abundance.

Writing As A Career

Beyond the personal rewards and satisfactions of writing lie major career opportunities.

The fact is that not every person *can* write, with expertness and skill. Of those who can, a smaller percentage are sufficiently talented to bring to their craft the gifts of imagination, style, and creativity. Of this smaller group, only the most fortunate have had the opportunities to experience life in its fullness, and to receive the rewards of insight, appreciation, and understanding that such a life can sometimes offer. Writers who are blessed with all three—skill, imagination, *and* experience—will often find themselves in a stimulating career filled not only with personal satisfactions, but rich rewards and even great fame.

While not every writer can be so fortunate, opportunities abound for them also.

Advertising agencies need copywriters. Publishers need editors. Newspapers need rewriters. Manufacturers and industrial companies need technical writers. Newsmagazines need journalists. The list of career opportunities for trained and competent writers is long, and growing.

At least equally important is the expanding need for writing skills among executives, administrators, and supervisors in career areas that may seem alien to the writer's expertise. The need to communicate—both verbally and in writing—is an urgent requirement in today's world of restive voters, suspicious customers, disillusioned stockholders, and frustrated employees. The ability to write effectively, accurately, and persuasively, from a solidly grounded value base, and with empathy and sensitivity, has become a much sought-after skill.

New career areas that directly or indirectly depend upon writing skills are opening daily.

Writing As Entertainment

We live in a world of increasing pressures, anxieties, and frustrations. The lightheartedness of decades past seems to have disappeared, along with its humor and simple down-to-earth forms of entertainment. Everything and everyone, it seems, now has a 'message.' The world impacts us with shattering and imponderable problems, and life seems terribly serious.

Seldom before has there been such an urgent need for people to be able to leave their troubles and problems behind, however temporarily, and to find respite in absorbing, wholesome entertainment.

Good writing can provide such entertainment. There must surely be a special place reserved in heaven for those delightful writers who, with their elfish natures and natural humor, are storytellers at heart, bringing suspense and joy to their audiences, young and old.

Writing As A Record of History

How many adults struggled during their childhood through the date-pocked courses of history—bored, disenchanted, waiting only for the end of that cobwebbed test of endurance—to find, in later years, that history was really the most fascinating and stimulating of all areas of knowledge? The number must be countless.

Why this unfortunate paradox? Did 'history' change? No! What changed was the presentation and the emphasis.

However important dates, names, and places may be to an expert understanding of history, they are not history, but merely the checkpoints and framework of history.

History is people—real people, with blood and bones, loves and hates, passions, strengths, and weaknesses. History is joys and sorrows, successes and failures, heartbreaks and ecstacies. And history is the pressure and tension of opposing forces, both in and out of balance. History is power, the exercise of power, and the vacuum of power.

The reinterpretation of history in such human terms has created major opportunities and needs for those skilled, sensitive, and tireless investigative writers whose training and interests incline them toward this important literary area.

The Writer As Interpreter of World Trends

World events of recent decades have moved with a dizzying speed leaving people everywhere in a state of shock—the dismemberment and decline of the British Empire; the emergence of the Third World with all its needs and problems; the struggle by blacks and other minorities for equality; the convolutions and realignments of the Cold War; the emergence of new nuclear powers; the influence of oil and other sources of energy on the economies of the world; major reinterpretations of family life, marriage, sex, religion, and social structures; the drug problem; the disastrous adventure in Southeast Asia; the explosive potential of the Middle East; the assasinations of presidents, would-be presidents, and beloved leaders; bussing and integration; crime and violence; the fundamental struggle between Left and Right, between Capitalism, Socialism, Communism, and Fascism; the massive impact of radio and television on the world's consciousness and awareness.

All of these events and pressures have left us breathless and confused. *What is happening to us? Where are we headed? What are the answers? Are there answers?*

The world has simply become too complex for the average person—already beleaguered by the pressures and requirements of his own life—to fully understand. Yet, day after day he is forced to make his decisions and cast his ballots on technical, scientific, political, and legal questions upon which even the experts, who have studied them for a lifetime, cannot agree.

The need for broadly educated journalists, reporters, and writers, gifted with insight and wisdom, and guided by the search for truth, who can energetically investigate, report, and interpret this kaleidoscope of world trends in terms each individual can understand and relate to, is urgent. It may, in fact, be a determining factor in the ability of democracy to survive as a viable system of government.

The Writer As Interpreter of Technology

Writers are people, and people are different. Each must write from the vantage point of his own character, personality, and experiences. Some will write as poets; others as artists. Still others as philosophers or historians.

But there is another kind of writer of importance—the technical writer. It is his task to be the communications bridge between the non-professional layman and the highly specialized scientific, medical, technological, and legal communities.

To achieve this demanding objective he must have much of the intellect and fundamental training of the disciplines involved. He must, in addition, possess that rare talent for simplifying the complex, without sacrificing the truth and accuracy of the original. He must have a mind that can view the complexities involved through the eye of the non-professional—a truly demanding combination of talents.

Every field of knowledge—even those once considered 'non-scientific'—is rapidly moving toward the quantifiable jurisdictions of science and mathematics. In the process, they become increasingly indecipherable to the non-scientific layman.

One of the more serious problems afflicting industry and the professions today is the widespread inability to effectively communicate. Millions of dollars and manhours are wasted each year because *managements do not take the time, or do not know how, to effectively communicate* their strategies, objectives, needs, problems, and reasons to increasingly sophisticated individuals who *must* be convinced, if there is to be any real hope for their accomplishment. It is just not enough, in a non-authoritative society and economy, to be able to dream great dreams or to solve difficult scientific and technological problems. Little of real consequence will be achieved without the understanding and the support of all those who must be called upon to implement those dreams and give them the breath of reality—associates, executives, investors, employees, voters, politicians, or other nations.

One of the important tasks of the technical writer is to provide such communication.

The Writer As Scientist

What is science? Is it not the unlocking of the mysteries and laws of nature, and the accurate interpretation of the truths thus discovered in ways that allow them to be repeated, proven, and used by mankind?

But *science does not create those laws*—it merely discovers and formularizes them. If, by some magical process, all of the infinite laws and facts that already exist throughout the universe could suddenly be made clear to us; if all of the elusive truths for which we search could be explained; if the destination toward which all of civilization is moving so agonizingly could suddenly be revealed—*what would science be then?*

If the true role of science and the scientist is that of verifiable discovery, then the writer of honor, skill, and caution, the seeker of truth, is equally and in every sense a scientist. Indeed, as traditional science approaches the end of its quest for mechanistic truths, it may well be that the subjective writer, seeking his own truths in new areas and directions, may bring benefits to mankind which can be discovered in no other way.

Ernest Nagel, Professor of Philosophy at Columbia University, has written:

> "It is well to recognize. . . that the science of man has not achieved, and may never achieve, such integrated systems of knowledge which are the pride of some of the modern natural sciences. Nor is it always possible, or for that matter desirable, to apply criteria of validity in the study of the human scene with the rigor customary in certain other disciplines."

There exists within us—in the depths of our minds and souls—a mysterious, uncharted frontier of new understanding. Some spend a lifetime plumbing its depths—each year moving one step deeper, attempting to shine the light of understanding into the dark and frightening crevices and canyons that await. Each year it seems that the bottom has at last been touched, only to find another unseen path leading deeper still. And we finally begin to wonder: *Is there an end, or does it go on forever?* But once the journey starts, the end no longer really matters. We continue because we *must!* For we sense the enormity of that which awaits—and *we must know!* And we guess that, whatever truths may lie outside—even to the stars—the *most important truths of all will be found within.* And something seems to say that *there lies God, and only there—deep, deep within us—will we find oneness with Him and all that He has created.*

This vast world exists, one may presume, within each of us. But the extent to which it is recognized and explored varies tremendously. Most, indeed, are so outwardly-oriented that observations of this kind seem absurd. There is no pretense in their position. Their lives are simply directed toward and controlled by a distinctly different sector of the mind's sphere. So, if this other world does exist for them, they are often unaware of it. At best it represents a dark continent which they feel should be left alone, undisturbed.

But for the writer-scientist, whose area of interest includes the elusive laws of the human condition, this never-ending journey *must be made.* And, slowly, *discoveries will be made and understandings will be arrived at which are available from no other laboratory.*

The Writer As Student of Human Nature

Spectacular advances in the fields of technology, medicine, and the physical sciences have been made during the past century, and especially the past half-century. Atomic power, nuclear fission, radar, penicillin, space exploration, computer science, television, communication satellites, and much, much more have all combined to form a new world for us all. We can now predict, with pin-point accuracy, what a space craft will do on the blind side of the moon. Yet, *we are little closer to predicting what man will or will not do under a given situation than were Plato or Aristotle in the days of ancient Greece.*

For all of its marvels, science has woefully failed to even understand, much less to predict, the secrets of the human soul, mind, emotions, innermost drives and conflicts, and value structure of a single thinking, feeling human being.

Yet, of all the needs and problems that inundate our world, none are more urgent than these distinctly human problems. The rapidly mounting incidence of crime, drugs, alcoholism, and mental disorders are no more than symptoms of far more serious and deeply-rooted causes that are afflicting societies everywhere.

But where are the answers? How can we understand and cope with those subtle, awful pressures that tend to direct our lives so silently, so uncontrollably? *No one yet knows.*

But one thing is certain. We cannot hope to delegate the responsibility for solving these human problems to any single discipline. *All of us* must contribute to the search. And slowly, very slowly no doubt, a *science of man* will finally begin to form. And individuals everywhere will at last begin to fully understand themselves, those around them, and the multitude of pressures that made them what they are and influence, so inexorably, that which they may become. Only then can man become, in fact, 'master of his fate and captain of his soul.'

Introspection and experiences—they are the grist of the writer's mill.

Absorb life! Every joy, every sorrow, every mountain too steep to climb, every success and frustration, every new scene and experience. Whether your heart is overflowing with happiness or your eyes are filled with tears, absorb it all. Record it all. Inculcate it all into the depths of your soul to mix with all that has gone before. *Finally, uncalled, it will return to you in new and usable form.*

Relish experiences, however simple and unimportant they may seem. Value them all, because bit by tiny bit they form the writer's insight, understanding, and wisdom upon which all his contributions will rest. And, added to those of your counterparts throughout the world, the problems that face mankind may one day be solved.

The Writer As Artist

An artist is defined as one who 'practices an imaginative art.' It is equally accurate to state that an artist is one who practices the communication of feelings and emotions—for they are the tools of his trade.

A painter is an artist, as is a musician and a dancer. Certainly, in this same sense, a writer is equally an artist, especially as his works transcend the world of the mundane toward that of the creative.

Few arts can approach the capacity of words to stir the emotions. Five hundred words can construct, in the mind, a set of lavish splendor which would otherwise cost thousands of dollars. The mind can be made to smell the vilest sewer, or meander through the most luxuriant forest—with words. Words can stimulate the most primitive desires, or the noblest aspirations. They can make the chest swell with pride, or the heart pain with empathy.

Deftly waved, the wand of words can bring us the magic of a world we would otherwise never experience. And *it is the writer who offers us this miracle.*

The Writer As Persuader

It is a truism of human nature that technical, scientific, and production-oriented specialists are rarely persuaders, at least by choice. The natural geniuses in such areas of expertise are, most often, completely absorbed in the challenges of their work. They deal in facts and figures, weights and measures, scientific laws and quantifiable 'things.' They are usually project-oriented, and when the project of their interest has been completed (i.e., solved, produced, or invented) their natural inclination is to move on, immediately, to new fields to conquer. Any diversion of their energies toward 'selling' their results is contrary to their character.

Yet, like it or not, *we live in a world of persuasion.* Few ideas, products, or individuals—in our competitive society— are so unique or overwhelmingly superior that they can be presented to prospective supporters on a take-it-or-leave-it basis. There is nearly always an alternative available which, when effectively presented, can fill the need instead, while the other gathers dust—unused and unrewarded.

The history of our society is filled with stories of geniuses who refused to sully themselves with such concerns—and died as paupers in the process.

But what is persuasion, really?

What it is not, as many seem to think, is some mystical form of hypnosis through which a charlatan 'cons' an unsuspecting buyer into accepting a worthless product or idea which he neither wants nor needs. Those days of high-pressure sales tactics and naive consumers have been gone, generally, for many years.

The fact is that *people do change their minds* on the basis of new and better ideas—even intelligent, hardheaded individuals who pride themselves on their 'sales resistance.' Such changes of previous positions in the light of new and better information are, in fact, one indication of a mature or maturing mind.

The art of persuasion is an essential ingredient in a free, democratic society. lt is as necessary as the arrogance of authoritarian directives is antagonistic. Free citizens and free consumers need—and demand—the right to consider all sides of each issue, and to make up—*or change*—their minds as facts warrant. *Persuasion is the thoughtful, empathic presentation of a product or idea which attempts to relate to the needs and desires of the individuals involved in an accurate, concise, and understandable manner.*

Persuasive writing, therefore, is a valuable form of communication which is in high demand in a free society, and which offers enormous rewards.

The Writer As A Bridge for Civilization

In many important respects, *man is the product of his experiences*—from the moment of birth to the time of death. Every exposure to other beings, to things, to events that surround and embrace him; every sensation of touch, sound, smell, sight, and taste—all combine into a synthesis of effect on what man is and will become. And with each new wave, man becomes different in some inscrutable way than he was the moment before.

Obviously, the intensity of these experiences varies tremendously, as do the effects. Some are so much a part of the daily routine that it may be impossible to recognize their effects; others will be so traumatic that each effect is deep, evident, and results in immediate and lasting changes in character, personality, or mental outlook.

Some experiences teach, through the addition of new facts to one's repertoire of knowledge. Other experiences enable man to relate, compare, analyze, and evaluate that knowledge to which he has been previously exposed. Still others seem to merely, but importantly, enable us to recognize and articulate those innate truths and values which apparently always rested there, waiting only for the gentle kiss of life.

Man is forever in a state of becoming, striving toward completeness as an individual. Certainly the immense contributions of direct, personal experiences must not be underrated. And if we mortals were destined to live forever, personal experiences might be quite enough—*but we are not*!

How many experiences can a life entertain? However many, they are but a grain of sand compared to the vast, endless panorama of mankind and his universe. If there were no bridge over this chasm between the parts and the whole, man would be destined to end his days on earth hardly more complete and fulfilled than when he started. And *each new generation would be faced with the bleak prospect of learning again those lessons which had already been learned, over and over, by their predecessors.*

But, thank God, there is a bridge which links those important lessons of the past to the present, which weaves each thread of the present with those of one's contemporaries into a strengthened fabric of modern knowledge, and stands ready to transport the total structure of man's collected knowledge and wisdom into the time-span of generations yet unborn. This bridge upon which modern civilization is increasingly reliant is the written word, especially—for reasons of permanence, referencing, organization, and depth—in the form of *books.*

The world of books! That magical doorway through which a single, isolated human being can step into a thousand lives and ten thousand experiences, none of which he would otherwise have known existed, much less with intimate awareness.

And the writer is the one upon whom this burden of responsibility—*and wonderful opportunity*—must fall. For what more important and fulfilling task could any individual wish?

The Writer As A Seeker of Truth

Probably the greatest strains imposed on mankind in recent years have occurred within the area of truth and values.

There was a time when right and wrong were clear and absolute concepts solidly grounded on broadly accepted guidelines. The question of values seldom arose because the answers seemed so simple and so obvious.

Suddenly this changed—in sex, in marriage, in religion and education, in politics and in justice. Suddenly man found himself in the bewildering position of having to *define his own values*, rather than simply accepting those of another age.

It has been, and still is, a difficult transition. And our contemporary society has been going through the most perplexing period of soul searching and value hunting that has faced mankind in modern history.

Man has entered a new phase of his development characterized by an acute awareness of his most essential essence as a human being. He is attempting, almost frantically, to *understand himself* in the totality of his being. He is trying, with all the honesty he can command, *to be himself*—his true self, his best self—and to allow his peers the unrestricted freedom to pursue this search themselves, in their own way, and in their own time. He is searching for ways in which he can relate, in meaningful ways, both to others in his society and to the structure of that society itself—in all its technological and economic complexities—*without dishonoring or disowning those other personal objectives.*

There was a time, not long ago, when man was certain that knowledge begets understanding, understanding begets wisdom, and wisdom assures happiness, harmony, and contentment. There was a time when we believed that, *somewhere*, there was a single Truth that would finally answer all the bewildering inconsistencies of existence.

Where is contentment? Where is happiness? What is truth? Must one return to the simplicity of obliviousness to find the peace of such values? Knowledge brings answers, but even more questions. Understanding brings not Truth, but *many truths*, often in opposition. In the end, all the facts and all the knowledge available to man do not silence the raging torrents within his soul.

So the search continues, and much of the responsibility and hope for its eventual resolution must inevitably fall upon the shoulders of sensitive, intuitive writers of the future who will take up the task as others reach the end of their own personal journeys.

* * *

Many years ago a professor of English admonished our class with these words: "The surest way to learn to write—is to *write!* Every day, without fail, spend at least fifteen minutes writing about *something.* It doesn't have to be always 'good.' It needn't always be 'important.' It may be simple and everyday. But WRITE!"

This is sound advice.

But every writer is different, and each must approach his own blank page in his own special way. Some write with mechanical precision, carefully tracing the steps of their tightly structured outline; others write from an emotionally charged base that will not tolerate restraints. Such writers find it impossible to create 'on schedule.' They are most productive when they write in spurts, waiting until their creative reservoir is filled to bursting. Then, once drained, they simply wait again—and hope.

Whatever the most effective way to write—whether by clock or mood, event or emotional explosion—surely all writers must agree that the act of writing, of facing and conquering that foreboding sheet time after time, is essential to the development of their art. What is not so commonly understood is that the reasons extend beyond the merits of practice and self-discipline.

The creative channels of the mind seem to function much like pipes filled with heavy viscous oils. It must be kept warm and moving. When the flow stops, and the oil cools, it tends to harden. Both heat and pressure are needed to cause the sludge to loosen and liquify, and for a rapid, easy flow to begin again.

Creative heat and determined pressure! Essential ingredients in writing.

The truly creative writer faces an agonizing conflict in values. He is immersed in a symphony of advice, with a single, persistent theme: *Write to sell!* He hears it in the classroom. He reads it in every book on writing technique, in every manual on how-to-get-published. He sees its overwhelming logic in every aspect of his daily life. It is solid, practical advice that should not be overlooked—*and he knows it!*

What are the benefits of a song unsung, an unseen work of art—or a manuscript that is never published, and never read?

But there is another truth. *Each of us is unique, and we must honor that uniqueness*—regardless of the economics of the day or the pressures of the marketplace.

Poetry, essays, short stories, however well-written and deserving of literary acclaim, are rarely salable to today's cost-strangled publishers. And creating for a graveyard of unpublished manuscripts involves frustrations that few writers can bear forever.

Yet, *the warmth and wisdom of the poem, the insights of the essay, the biting succinctness of the well-structured short story are all important.* They are important to the orderly development of the writer's skill. They are important to the wounds and turmoil within the reader's soul. They are important to a civilization being wafted away on the wings of neatly packaged, myopic entertainment.

* * *

Whatever you write, no matter how you choose to write it—*write.*

It is important to our society and to civilization itself that each of us, with something of significance to share, make our own special contribution.

We learn from everyone, and each has something different to offer from all the rest. None of us has all the answers, but each can add his share to the greatness of the whole.

Too often those blessed with the greatest gifts, with the greatest insights and the most of value to be told, are least prone to do so. Their truths are locked within their ingenious minds and buried with them.

Do not let this happen to you! We need you . . . especially you. Now, before your time, too, has passed.

Appendix A

Pricing Tables

T he pricing tables that follow are provided for help in budgeting, specification, and scope of work decisions. They include plates and platemaking, presswork, paper, and bindery. They do not include typesetting, paging, negatives, veloxes, or halftones for photographs.

All prices are **List Prices** and are subject to resale discounts where applicable.

Base Specifications

Prices are for camera ready jobs with inside sheets printed on 60 lb. white uncoated book paper in black ink. *Perfect Bound* prices include covers printed on 65 lb. white coated-one-side cover paper printed in black ink. *Hardback* prices include covers produced from Kivar 5, embossed in gold or silver foil on the front and spine, Smythe sewn.

Additional charges for alternative papers and ink requirements are indicated on the table titled 'Additional Charges for Special Papers & Inks.'

Explanation of Terms

White Uncoated Book Paper. A good, basic, white paper, stocked by our company in 60 lb. weight, usually used for books that are primarily textual in nature without large numbers of halftones.

Natural Acid-Free Paper. A beautiful, high-quality paper, stocked by our company in 60 lb. weight and off-white color, usually used for books requiring very long life without the deterioration which can develop due to the acid content of some papers. Especially recommended for family, church, and county histories. The off-white color tends to accentuate the historical nature of such books. The paper takes photographs well, although without the snap and sparkle that come from the use of coated papers.

White Coated Matte Paper. A premium, high-quality paper, stocked by our company in 60 and 70 lb. weights, especially recommended for books involving many professionally-prepared photographs. The matte (suede) finish provides the many advantages of coated papers without the glare problem associated with high-gloss enamels.

Coated-One-Side Cover Paper. An excellent, semi-gloss, economy-grade white cover paper which is very durable and attractive and stocked by our company in 10 point thickness. While not having the mirror-finish of Kromekote, the addition of plastic coatings over the ink can provide such gloss.

Antique Finish Cover Paper. A 65 lb. uncoated cover paper which is available in a wide range of attractive colors, including white.

Cordwain Cover Paper. A 90 lb. uncoated cover paper which features a leather-embossed, hard finish. It is very durable and is available in a wide range of attractive colors, including white.

Kromekote Cover Paper. A high prestige cover paper which features a mirror-finish. It is stocked by our company in white, 10 point, coated-one-side.

Var. (Varnish) An additional press run which applies a coating of varnish over all other inks used. Helps to avoid ink smears and scratches. Usually used when ink colors other than black are specified.

Plastic Laminates. Sheets of plastic which are sometimes used, instead of varnish, to provide extra protection and gloss to covers for perfect bound books.

UV Liquid Plastic Laminates. An additional press run which applies a coating of liquid plastic over all other inks used. Final sheets are transported through a heat tunnel equipped with ultraviolet lamps which heat-set the plastic. The final result is an extraordinarily beautiful, very high gloss finish which provides extra protection to covers of perfect bound books.

HC/CR/BLD. (Heavy coverage, close register, bleeds.) Concerns the inks and printing requirements for covers on perfect bound books. Each of these requirements demand slower press speeds, more preparation time, and, consequently, somewhat higher costs.

4 Color + Varnish + Separations. Concerns the full-color treatment of covers for perfect bound books. Charges include the four ink colors used plus varnish plus the cost of negative separations.

LIST PRICE TABLE
Perfect Bound Books—5½″ x 8½″
(Price Per Book)

Pages	250	500	1000	2000	3000	4000	5000	Add'l
64	4.12	2.30	1.42	1.02	.90	.84	.77	.51
80	4.49	2.53	1.57	1.13	.99	.92	.85	.57
96	4.92	2.78	1.74	1.26	1.11	1.03	.95	.63
112	5.33	3.03	1.91	1.39	1.23	1.14	1.05	.71
128	5.74	3.29	2.08	1.52	1.34	1.25	1.16	.79
144	6.15	3.54	2.24	1.64	1.46	1.36	1.26	.86
160	6.56	3.79	2.41	1.77	1.57	1.47	1.36	.94
176	6.99	4.06	2.60	1.92	1.70	1.60	1.49	1.06
192	7.42	4.33	2.78	2.07	1.84	1.73	1.62	1.18
208	7.85	4.60	2.97	2.21	1.97	1.86	1.75	1.30
224	8.28	4.87	3.16	2.36	2.10	1.99	1.87	1.42
240	8.27	5.14	3.35	2.51	2.24	2.12	2.00	1.54
256	9.15	5.40	3.53	2.66	2.37	2.25	2.13	1.65
272	9.58	5.67	3.72	2.81	2.50	2.38	2.26	1.77
288	10.01	5.94	3.91	2.95	2.63	2.51	2.39	1.89
304	10.44	6.21	4.09	3.10	2.77	2.64	2.52	2.01
320	10.87	6.48	4.28	3.25	2.90	2.77	2.64	2.13
336	11.36	6.77	4.47	3.40	3.03	2.90	2.77	2.24
352	11.86	7.07	4.67	3.55	3.17	3.03	2.90	2.35
368	12.35	7.36	4.86	3.70	3.30	3.16	3.01	2.42
384	12.84	7.65	5.06	3.85	3.44	3.28	3.12	2.50
400	13.33	7.95	5.25	4.00	3.57	3.40	3.23	2.57
416	13.83	8.24	5.44	4.15	3.70	3.53	3.35	2.64
432	14.32	8.53	5.64	4.30	3.84	3.65	3.46	2.71
448	14.81	8.83	5.83	4.45	3.97	3.77	3.57	2.78
464	15.30	9.12	6.02	4.59	4.10	3.89	3.69	2.85
480	15.80	9.41	6.22	4.74	4.24	4.02	3.80	2.92
496	16.29	9.70	6.41	4.89	4.37	4.14	3.91	2.99
512	16.78	10.00	6.61	5.04	4.51	4.26	4.02	3.06
528	17.27	10.29	6.80	5.19	4.64	4.39	4.14	3.14
544	17.77	10.58	6.99	5.34	4.77	4.51	4.25	3.21
560	18.26	10.88	7.19	5.49	4.91	4.63	4.36	3.28
576	18.75	11.17	7.38	5.64	5.04	4.75	4.45	3.27

			LIST PRICE TABLE					
			Perfect Bound Books—6″ x 9″					
			(Price Per Book)					
Pages	**250**	**500**	**1000**	**2000**	**3000**	**4000**	**5000**	**Add'l**
64	4.18	2.36	1.47	1.06	.94	.88	.81	.55
80	4.57	2.59	1.63	1.18	1.04	.97	.90	.62
96	5.01	2.86	1.81	1.32	1.17	1.09	1.01	.69
112	5.44	3.12	1.99	1.46	1.30	1.21	1.12	.78
128	5.86	3.39	2.17	1.60	1.42	1.33	1.24	.87
144	6.29	3.65	2.34	1.74	1.55	1.45	1.35	.95
160	6.71	3.91	2.52	1.88	1.67	1.57	1.46	1.04
176	7.16	4.19	2.72	2.04	1.81	1.70	1.59	1.14
192	7.60	4.47	2.92	2.19	1.95	1.84	1.72	1.25
208	8.05	4.75	3.11	2.35	2.10	1.97	1.85	1.35
224	8.49	5.03	3.31	2.51	2.24	2.11	1.98	1.45
240	8.94	5.32	3.51	2.67	2.38	2.24	2.11	1.56
256	9.39	5.60	3.71	2.82	2.52	2.38	2.23	1.66
272	9.83	5.88	3.91	2.98	2.66	2.51	2.36	1.76
288	10.28	6.16	4.10	3.14	2.81	2.65	2.49	1.86
304	10.72	6.44	4.30	3.29	2.95	2.78	2.62	1.97
320	11.17	6.72	4.50	3.45	3.09	2.92	2.75	2.07
336	11.68	7.03	4.71	3.61	3.23	3.06	2.89	2.21
352	12.18	7.33	4.92	3.77	3.38	3.21	3.04	2.35
368	12.69	7.64	5.12	3.93	3.52	3.34	3.16	2.45
384	13.20	7.95	5.33	4.09	3.67	3.48	3.29	2.54
400	13.70	8.25	5.54	4.25	3.81	3.62	3.42	2.64
416	14.21	8.56	5.75	4.41	3.96	3.75	3.55	2.73
432	14.71	8.87	5.95	4.57	4.10	3.89	3.68	2.83
448	15.22	9.18	6.16	4.74	4.25	4.02	3.80	2.92
464	15.73	9.48	6.37	4.90	4.39	4.16	3.93	3.02
480	16.23	9.79	6.58	5.06	4.53	4.30	4.06	3.12
496	16.74	10.10	6.78	5.22	4.68	4.43	4.19	3.21
512	17.25	10.40	6.99	5.38	4.82	4.57	4.32	3.31
528	17.75	10.71	7.20	5.54	4.97	4.71	4.45	3.40
544	18.26	11.02	7.41	5.70	5.11	4.84	4.57	3.50
560	18.76	11.32	7.61	5.86	5.26	4.98	4.70	3.59
576	19.27	11.63	7.82	6.02	5.40	5.10	4.80	3.60

LIST PRICE TABLE
Perfect Bound Books—8½″ x 11″
(Price Per Book)

Pages	250	500	1000	2000	3000	4000	5000	Add'l
64	5.40	3.15	2.03	1.52	1.36	1.28	1.20	.88
80	6.06	3.56	2.31	1.75	1.56	1.47	1.38	1.02
96	6.71	3.96	2.59	1.97	1.76	1.66	1.56	1.16
112	7.50	4.45	2.93	2.24	2.01	1.90	1.79	1.34
128	8.28	4.94	3.28	2.52	2.26	2.13	2.01	1.52
144	9.07	5.42	3.62	2.79	2.50	2.37	2.24	1.70
160	9.85	5.91	3.96	3.06	2.75	2.61	2.46	1.88
176	10.73	6.44	4.32	3.34	3.01	2.85	2.69	2.05
192	11.61	6.98	4.68	3.62	3.26	3.09	2.92	2.23
208	12.49	7.51	5.04	3.91	3.52	3.33	3.14	2.40
224	13.37	8.04	5.40	4.19	3.77	3.57	3.37	2.58
240	14.26	8.58	5.76	4.47	4.03	3.81	3.60	2.75
256	15.14	9.11	6.12	4.75	4.28	4.05	3.83	2.92
272	16.02	9.64	6.48	5.03	4.54	4.30	4.06	3.10
288	16.90	10.17	6.84	5.32	4.79	4.54	4.28	3.27
304	17.78	10.71	7.20	5.60	5.05	4.78	4.51	3.45
320	18.66	11.24	7.56	5.88	5.30	5.02	4.74	3.62
336	19.54	11.77	7.92	6.16	5.56	5.28	5.00	3.88
352	20.42	12.31	8.28	6.45	5.81	5.53	5.25	4.13
368	21.30	12.84	8.64	6.73	6.07	5.77	5.48	4.31
384	22.18	13.37	9.00	7.01	6.32	6.01	5.71	4.49
400	23.06	13.90	9.36	7.29	6.58	6.26	5.94	4.66
416	23.94	14.44	9.72	7.58	6.83	6.50	6.17	4.84
432	24.82	14.97	10.08	7.86	7.09	6.74	6.39	5.01
448	25.71	15.50	10.44	8.14	7.34	6.98	6.62	5.19
464	26.59	16.03	10.80	8.42	7.60	7.22	6.85	5.37
480	27.47	16.57	11.16	8.71	7.85	7.47	7.08	5.54
496	28.35	17.10	11.52	8.99	8.11	7.71	7.31	5.72
512	29.23	17.63	11.88	9.27	8.36	7.95	7.54	5.90
528	30.11	18.16	12.24	9.55	8.62	8.19	7.77	6.07
544	30.99	18.70	12.60	9.84	8.87	8.43	8.00	6.25
560	31.87	19.23	12.96	10.12	9.13	8.67	8.22	6.42
576	32.75	19.76	13.32	10.40	9.38	8.89	8.40	6.44

LIST PRICE TABLE
Hardback Books—5½″ x 8½″
(Price Per Book)

Pages	250	500	1000	2000	3000	4000	5000	Add'l
64	6.70	4.30	3.01	2.41	2.21	2.13	2.05	1.73
80	7.08	4.53	3.16	2.52	2.31	2.22	2.14	1.80
96	7.45	4.75	3.31	2.63	2.40	2.31	2.22	1.86
112	7.93	5.06	3.52	2.79	2.54	2.45	2.35	1.97
128	8.41	5.37	3.73	2.95	2.69	2.58	2.48	2.07
144	8.89	5.67	3.93	3.10	2.83	2.72	2.61	2.18
160	9.37	5.98	4.14	3.26	2.97	2.86	2.74	2.28
176	9.85	6.29	4.35	3.42	3.11	2.99	2.87	2.38
192	10.33	6.60	4.56	3.58	3.26	3.13	3.00	2.49
208	10.80	6.91	4.76	3.74	3.40	3.26	3.13	2.59
224	11.28	7.22	4.97	3.90	3.54	3.40	3.26	2.70
240	11.76	7.53	5.18	4.06	3.69	3.54	3.39	2.80
256	12.24	7.83	5.39	4.22	3.83	3.67	3.52	2.90
272	12.72	8.14	5.60	4.38	3.97	3.81	3.65	3.01
288	13.19	8.45	5.80	4.54	4.11	3.95	3.78	3.11
304	13.67	8.76	6.01	4.70	4.26	4.08	3.91	3.22
320	14.15	9.07	6.22	4.86	4.40	4.22	4.04	3.32
336	14.67	9.41	6.45	5.03	4.55	4.38	4.20	3.48
352	15.19	9.76	6.68	5.21	4.71	4.53	4.35	3.64
368	15.71	10.10	6.90	5.38	4.86	4.68	4.49	3.75
384	16.23	10.44	7.13	5.55	5.02	4.82	4.63	3.86
400	16.75	10.79	7.36	5.72	5.17	4.97	4.77	3.96
416	17.27	11.13	7.59	5.90	5.33	5.12	4.91	4.07
432	17.79	11.47	7.81	6.07	5.48	5.26	5.05	4.18
448	18.32	11.82	8.04	6.24	5.64	5.41	5.19	4.29
464	18.84	12.16	8.27	6.41	5.79	5.56	5.33	4.40
480	19.36	12.50	8.50	6.59	5.94	5.71	5.47	4.51
496	19.88	12.84	8.72	6.76	6.10	5.85	5.61	4.62
512	20.40	13.19	8.95	6.93	6.25	6.00	5.75	4.73
528	20.92	13.53	9.18	7.10	6.41	6.15	5.88	4.84
544	21.44	13.87	9.41	7.28	6.56	6.29	6.02	4.95
560	21.96	14.22	9.63	7.45	6.72	6.44	6.16	5.06
576	22.48	14.56	9.86	7.62	6.87	6.57	6.27	5.07

LIST PRICE TABLE
Hardback Books—6″ x 9″
(Price Per Book)

Pages	250	500	1000	2000	3000	4000	5000	Add'l
64	6.85	4.41	3.12	2.51	2.31	2.23	2.15	1.83
80	7.24	4.65	3.28	2.63	2.42	2.35	2.25	1.84
96	7.62	4.88	3.44	2.75	2.52	2.46	2.34	1.86
112	8.12	5.20	3.66	2.92	2.67	2.58	2.48	2.10
128	8.61	5.53	3.88	3.09	2.83	2.72	2.62	2.21
144	9.11	5.85	4.09	3.26	2.98	2.87	2.76	2.33
160	9.60	6.17	4.31	3.43	3.13	3.02	2.90	2.44
176	10.10	6.49	4.53	3.60	3.29	3.16	3.04	2.55
192	10.61	6.81	4.75	3.77	3.44	3.31	3.18	2.67
208	11.11	7.14	4.97	3.94	3.60	3.46	3.32	2.78
224	11.61	7.46	5.19	4.11	3.75	3.61	3.46	2.89
240	12.12	7.78	5.41	4.29	3.91	3.76	3.61	3.01
256	12.62	8.10	5.63	4.46	4.06	3.90	3.75	3.12
272	13.12	8.42	5.85	4.63	4.22	4.05	3.89	3.23
288	13.62	8.75	6.07	4.80	4.37	4.20	4.03	3.34
304	14.13	9.07	6.29	4.97	4.53	4.35	4.17	3.46
320	14.63	9.39	6.51	5.14	4.68	4.50	4.31	3.57
336	15.17	9.75	6.75	5.33	4.85	4.67	4.48	3.75
352	15.70	10.11	7.00	5.52	5.02	4.84	4.65	3.93
368	16.24	10.47	7.24	5.70	5.19	5.00	4.81	4.05
384	16.77	10.83	7.49	5.89	5.36	5.16	4.96	4.18
400	17.31	11.19	7.73	6.08	5.53	5.32	5.12	4.30
416	17.84	11.55	7.98	6.27	5.70	5.48	5.27	4.42
432	18.38	11.91	8.22	6.45	5.87	5.65	5.43	4.55
448	18.91	12.27	8.47	6.64	6.04	5.81	5.58	4.67
464	19.45	12.63	8.71	6.83	6.20	5.97	5.74	4.80
480	19.98	12.99	8.95	7.02	6.37	6.13	5.89	4.92
496	20.52	13.35	9.20	7.20	6.54	6.29	6.04	5.05
512	21.05	13.71	9.44	7.39	6.71	6.46	6.20	5.17
528	21.59	14.07	9.69	7.58	6.88	6.62	6.35	5.29
544	22.12	14.43	9.93	7.77	7.05	6.78	6.51	5.42
560	22.66	14.79	10.18	7.95	7.22	6.94	6.66	5.54
576	23.19	15.15	10.42	8.14	7.39	7.09	6.78	5.56

				LIST PRICE TABLE				
			Hardback Books—8½″ x 11″					
			(Price Per Book)					
Pages	**250**	**500**	**1000**	**2000**	**3000**	**4000**	**5000**	**Add'l**
64	9.09	6.46	4.58	3.71	3.42	3.31	3.19	2.73
80	9.75	6.87	4.85	3.92	3.61	3.48	3.36	2.87
96	10.41	7.27	5.12	4.13	3.79	3.66	3.53	3.01
112	11.31	7.85	5.51	4.43	4.07	3.92	3.78	3.21
128	12.21	8.43	5.91	4.74	4.34	4.19	4.03	3.41
144	13.10	9.01	6.30	5.04	4.62	4.45	4.28	3.61
160	14.00	9.59	6.69	5.34	4.89	4.71	4.53	3.81
176	14.92	10.20	7.11	5.66	5.18	4.98	4.79	4.00
192	15.84	10.81	7.52	5.98	5.47	5.26	5.04	4.19
208	16.75	11.42	7.94	6.30	5.76	5.53	5.30	4.38
224	17.67	12.03	8.35	6.62	6.05	5.80	5.56	4.57
240	18.59	12.65	8.77	6.95	6.34	6.08	5.82	4.77
256	19.51	13.26	9.18	7.27	6.63	6.35	6.07	4.96
272	20.43	13.87	9.60	7.59	6.92	6.62	6.33	5.15
288	21.34	14.48	10.01	7.91	7.21	6.90	6.59	5.34
304	22.26	15.09	10.43	8.23	7.50	7.17	6.84	5.53
320	23.18	15.70	10.84	8.55	7.79	7.45	7.10	5.72
336	24.06	16.28	11.23	8.85	8.06	7.72	7.38	6.03
352	24.94	16.85	11.62	9.15	8.33	7.99	7.66	6.32
368	25.83	17.43	12.01	9.45	8.60	8.25	7.91	6.54
384	26.71	18.01	12.40	9.75	8.87	8.51	8.16	6.75
400	27.59	18.58	12.79	10.05	9.14	8.77	8.41	6.96
416	28.47	19.16	13.18	10.35	9.41	9.03	8.66	7.17
432	29.35	19.73	13.57	10.65	9.68	9.29	8.91	7.39
448	30.24	20.31	13.96	10.95	9.95	9.55	9.16	7.60
464	31.12	20.89	14.34	11.25	10.21	9.81	9.41	7.81
480	32.00	21.46	14.73	11.55	10.48	10.07	9.66	8.03
496	32.88	22.04	15.12	11.85	10.75	10.33	9.91	8.24
512	33.76	22.62	15.51	12.15	11.02	10.59	10.17	8.45
528	34.64	23.19	15.90	12.45	11.29	10.85	10.42	8.66
544	35.53	23.77	16.29	12.75	11.56	11.11	10.67	8.88
560	36.41	24.34	16.68	13.05	11.83	11.37	10.92	9.09
576	37.29	24.92	17.07	13.35	12.10	11.61	11.11	9.13

<table>
<tr><th colspan="9" style="text-align:center">ADDITIONAL PRICES
For Special Papers & Inks</th></tr>
<tr><th>DESCRIPTION</th><th>250</th><th>500</th><th>1000</th><th>2000</th><th>3000</th><th>4000</th><th>5000</th><th>A/M</th></tr>
</table>

DESCRIPTION	250	500	1000	2000	3000	4000	5000	A/M
INSIDE PAPERS								
5½″ x 8½″ Books	(Additional Charges/Book/16 pages)							
60lb. Acid Free Natural	.03	.02	.02	.02	.02	.02	.02	.02
60lb. Coated White-Matte	.06	.04	.04	.03	.03	.03	.03	.03
70lb. Coated White-Matte	.07	.05	.04	.04	.04	.04	.04	.03
6″ x 9″ Books	(Additional Charges/Book/16 pages)							
60lb. Acid Free Natural	.03	.02	.02	.02	.02	.02	.02	.02
60lb. Coated White-Matte	.06	.04	.04	.03	.03	.03	.03	.03
70lb. Coated White-Matte	.07	.05	.04	.04	.04	.04	.04	.03
8½″ x 11″ Books	(Additional Charges/Book/16 pages)							
60lb. Acid Free Natural	.03	.02	.02	.02	.02	.02	.02	.02
60lb. Coated White-Matte	.06	.04	.04	.03	.03	.03	.03	.03
70lb. Coated White-Matte	.07	.05	.04	.04	.04	.04	.04	.03
COATED PAPERS								
5½″ x 8½″ Books	(Additional Charges/Book)							
Carnival Antique 65lb.	.06	.05	.05	.04	.04	.04	.04	.04
Carnival Cordwain 90lb.	.07	.06	.06	.05	.05	.05	.05	.05
Kromkote 10 pt. C1S	.07	.07	.07	.06	.05	.05	.05	.05
6″ x 9″ Books	(Additional Charges/Book)							
Carnival Antique 65lb.	.06	.05	.05	.04	.04	.04	.04	.04
Carnival Cordwain 90lb.	.07	.06	.06	.05	.05	.05	.05	.05
Kromkote 10 pt. C1S	.07	.07	.07	.06	.05	.05	.05	.05
8½″ x 11″ Books	(Additional Charges/Book)							
Carnival Antique 65lb.	.12	.10	.10	.09	.08	.08	.08	.08
Carnival Cordwain 90lb.	.14	.12	.12	.11	.10	.10	.10	.10
Kromkote 10 pt. C1S	.16	.14	.14	.12	.11	.10	.10	.10
COVER INKS	(Additional Charges/Book)							
Black Ink-Inside	.45	.25	.18	.12	.10	.09	.08	.06
1 PMS+Var w/o HC/CR/BLD	.63	.79	.44	.26	.20	.17	.15	.07
2 PMS+Var w/o HC/CR/BLD	.76	.95	.53	.31	.24	.20	.18	.09
2 PMS+Varnish	1.26	1.58	.89	.52	.39	.33	.29	.15
3 PMS+Varnish	1.29	1.61	.94	.59	.47	.41	.38	.24
4 Color+Varnish+Separations	2.40	2.99	1.64	.96	.74	.63	.56	.29

Appendix B

Cost Saving Tips

Optical Scanning

This equipment system optically scans typeset or typewritten materials without the need for manual keyboarding. The results are then stored on 5¼" floppy disks or 8" phototypsetting disks. The original sheets to be scanned may be fed manually or automatically into the scanner, depending on the condition of the originals themselves.

The scanner is equipped with an artifical intelligence which allows it to be 'trained' to read a wide variety of type sizes and faces. A 'training set' must be developed on each new job to be scanned. However, training sets can be saved for future use.

Limitations. The originals to be scanned must be 'optically readable,' meaning that the images must consist of solid characters of consistent density with enough space between lines to avoid confusing the scanner in its attempts at character identification. It will not read dot matrix hardcopy from a computer, handwritten copy or material set in less than 9 point type.

Important. Pictures, art work, etc., must not be interspersed within the material to be scanned. All off-size material to be scanned should be firmly mounted on letter- or legal-sized sheets for automatic feeding.

Pricing. There is a $12.50 charge to develop a simple training set. More complex training sets will take longer and cost more.

The scanning charge for work to be produced will depend entirely on the scannability, complexity, and number of lines per page of the work involved.

The optimum specification for work to be scanned consists of an 8½"x 11" typewritten manuscript page produced on an electric typewriter using one-time ribbon, double spaced with 1" margins all around, without special formatting, type size or type face requirements. Such pages can be automatically fed into the scanner and cost $.50 to $1.00 per page, plus the cost of the training set. If the originals cannot be fed automatically, our minimum scanning charge is $1.50 per page.

However, as complexities are introduced into the originals to be scanned, the scanning speed (and accuracy) declines, and the time required for developing a training set increases.

For example, a single-spaced typewritten manuscript scans at a 50% slower speed than a double-spaced manuscript, which increases the scanning charge to about $2.00 per page, when auto-feeding can be used.

Manuscripts with superscript footnote references, underlining, etc., scan at a much slower speed, often increasing the basic scanning charge by $.50 per page, or more.

Typeset originals, involving several type size and type face changes require much longer to develop a training set and scan at a much slower speed, often increasing the charge required by $1.00 to $3.00 per page, or more.

While typeset tabular and statistical tables can be scanned, the time and charges involved rarely make it a cost-effective application.

Our minimum charge per job is $25.00.

Accuracy & Error Correction. The accuracy level achievable on this system is directly related to the quality and complexity of the material to be scanned.

Manuscripts produced to the optimum specification (as described above) will have an accuracy rate of about 95 percent. As the complexities of superscripts, underlines, size changes, face changes, etc., are introduced, this accuracy level drops.

Scanning charges, as explained above, *do not include error correction or typographic formatting by scanner operators.* Such corrections can be made in a more time-effective manner on word processing equipment.

If error correction by scanner operators is required, additional editing charges will be made at standard hourly rates based on the actual editing time required.

In all cases, the most satisfactory procedure to be followed on new jobs is to let us run a time test on a cross section of the work to be produced before prices are quoted.

DEST Scanning

This system scans both text and graphics materials and stores the results on either a 5¼" floppy disk or onto a computer hard disk. Originals must be typewritten or from a laser printer. Graphic materials may be either line art or continuous tone photographs. Originals must be fed manually into the scanner.

Limitations. Unlike the optical scanner, the DEST Scanner has no artificial intelligence, cannot be trained, and does not require that a traning set be developed. For the most part, it will either scan the material presented or it won't. There is no in-between.

It will not scan typeset originals or originals set in different type sizes and type faces. Continuous tone photographs to be scanned can only be produced in 300 dots per inch print resolution.

Advantages. While the DEST Scanner is much less versatile than the optical scanner, what it can do it does extraordinarily well and with exceptional accuracy.

Scanned text files can be saved directly to a .DOC file which can immediately be edited with MicroSoft Word software. It also does a superior job of scanning typewritten or laser printed tables and statistical matter, both of which can also be immediately edited on MicroSoft Word software.

An especially useful application involves the preparation of complex statistical tables on a spread sheet (such as SuperCalc), printing out the resultant table on a laser printer, scanning that table on the DEST Scanner, editing or adding non-tabular information on MicroSoft Word, and then formatting and printing the final results on a desktop publishing system such as Ventura.

Pricing. While the standard hourly rate for this equipment is less than that of the optical scanner, it scans at a much slower speed. Therefore, scanning charges are about the same.

Both line art and continuous tone photographs scan at an even slower speed and cost $3.00 to $5.00 per individual sheet scanned.

Our minimum charge per job is $15.00

Accuracy & Error Correction. Charges *do not include error correction or typographic formatting by scanner operators.* Such corrections can be made in a more time-effective manner by the client or by others on word processing equipment.

If error correction by scanner operators is required, additional editing charges will be made at standard hourly rates based on the actual time required.

The most satisfactory procedure to be followed on new jobs is to run a time test on a cross section of the material to be produced before prices are quoted.

Computer-Controlled Halftone Camera

This equipment system produces high quality positive veloxes and positive screened halftones in the most time- and cost-effective manner possible. It is computer-controlled with a built-in densitometer for reading and setting values for producing halftones.

Within the limitations of the copyboard and film sizes, originals can be reduced to 25 percent or enlarged to 200 percent of original size. Receiver film sizes of 8½" x 11" and 12" x 18" are available.

Both black-and-white and color originals can be processed. However, photographs involving significant amounts of both red and black require the use of panchromatic film.

Halftone screens of 85, 100, 120, and 133 lines are available.

Limitations. This system does not produce reverses and cannot effectively handle overlays or callouts involving overlays.

PRICE TABLE

Size	Veloxes	Halftones
3" x 5"	$4.00 each	$ 6.00 each
4" x 6"	$5.00 each	$ 8.50 each
6" x 9"	$6.00 each	$ 9.00 each
8" x 10"	$7.00 each	$10.00 each

Increase all prices 100% for gang shots. Increase halftone prices 80% for use of panchromatic film.

Sizing. All prices assume that sizing percentages have been computed and furnished by the client. If not, add $.75 per illustration for sizing.

Waxing. Add $.50 per illustration for the application of adhesive wax.

Minimum Charge. $10.00 per order.

Phototypesetting

We use the Varitype 6400 Comp/Edit Phototypesetting System with two image previewers and three off-line Varityper 5618 input terminals. (We also input and/or edit manuscripts on five AT&T 6300 computers with 20mb hard disks using MicroSoft Word software.) Type point sizes from 5½ points through 72 points can be produced, with line lengths up to 45 picas.

We carry a large inventory of type families which are more than adequate for books and manuals which we specialize in. Additional families of type can be added as needed. All type may be produced 'straight' or may be custom-kerned, condensed, expanded or slanted, as required. Both foreign language and special accent fonts are also carried.

Type is output on resin coated photographic paper in 8 inch wide galleys which are then developed, fixed, washed and dried in a continuous processor, ready for proofing.

We use three different sources for setting type:

1. Manuscripts can be manually keystroked using the 6400 keyboard or terminals.
2. Manuscripts can be optically scanned, translated into typographic language with out Shaffstall MediaCom onto an 8″ phototypesetting disk, then coded, edited and output on the 6400.
3. Manuscripts can be received on IBM PC compatible 5¼″ floppy computer disks, and then transmitted through the Shaffstall MediaCom onto a phototypesetting disk and output on the 6400.

We usually find it most time- and cost-effective to utilize two or more of these systems on each job.

Pricing. Work may be priced by either:

1. estimating the amount of time that will be required to produce it and multiplying that time by our standard hourly rates for the equipment involved, or
2. by counting the characters involved and multiplying the total character count by the appropriate selling price per thousand characters.

Most text copy can be priced by the 'character count' method. While this is necessarily a subjective approach, it can be quite accurate if the work to be done is realistically and accurately evaluated as to the complexities involved.

We divide work into 6 complexity levels, with Level #1 being the simplest and fastest, and Level #6 being the most complex and time consuming.

Level #1 anticipates basically 'straight' typesetting with no more than 2 different formats, a minimum number of type face and type size changes, no outline, tabular work or indents, and few heads or subheads.

This level of work is priced at $7.00 per 1000 characters, when keystroking is done by our operators on our Varityper terminals.

Level #6 anticipates typesetting which involves many different changes, type face and size changes, outlines and/or multiple indents, many heads and subheads, footnote superscript references, some simple formulas, some words in foreign language, etc.

This level of work is priced at $12.00 per 1000 characters, when keystroking is done by our operators on our Varityper terminals.

Levels #2 through #5 are the most difficult to define in that they usually involve subtle increases in the amount of complexity. When the job is large, it is usually a good idea to let us run a time-test on two or three manuscript pages.

PRICE TABLE

Level #1	$7.00/M Characters
Level #2	$8.00/M Characters
Level #3	$9.00/M Characters
Level #4	$9.50/M Characters
Level #5	$10.80/M Characters
Level #6	$12.00/M Characters

Significant price reductions can be given on typesetting when the work can either be scanned on our optical scanner or is furnished to us on an IBM PC compatible floppy disk. However, before arbitrarily passing on such discounts, we must be certain about the complexities involved.

For example, for the lowest possible price available for work which can be scanned, manuscripts must precisely conform to our optimum specifications defined earlier in this section. If it doesn't, the time involved will increase and price reduction will decrease.

Work provided on a computer disk must be tested to ensure that unnecessary 'garbage' removal and tedious formatting problems are not involved.

Client Involvement. With the ever increasing use of computers, word processors, desktop publishing software, scanners, etc.,

illustrations are involved, there will be an additional laydown for each illustration, and a laydown for each caption if included. On larger page sizes, two or more columns may be involved which not only increases the number of laydowns but also slows the pagination process since the columns must be aligned with one another.

Today, however, books are rarely paged manually. Our company uses an electronic pagination system which is cost-effective for most fixed-format jobs. Pagination is performed on the Varityper 6400 and hand pagination is virtually eliminated.

For the 6400 to produce copy in paginated form, special typographic commands must be embedded. They can either be added on the Varityper or may be embedded on a computer while the manuscript is still on the word processor. If the commands are embedded accurately, the job can be processed without manual intervention and will print out in final paginated form, with sequential page numbers and running heads, ready for negatives and/or presswork.

Pricing. The most costly and time consuming aspects of manual pagination are not the laydowns themselves, but the time involved in subjective and creative judgments. *This is especially true of newsletters, brochures, etc., where pagination time can double or triple the time required for fixed-format books and manuals.*

When all pagination data is accurately and completely embedded within the text, galleys can be bypassed and minimum pagination cost is involved. When pagination must be done by hand, additional charges are involved.

A layout artist can complete an average of 20 laydowns per hour which makes our basic manual layout price about $2.00 per laydown. When additional laydowns are involved, this charge obviously must be increased. We increase final layout prices by 25% for multi-column pagination. When subjective or creative judgments are required, prices must be increased accordingly.

Glossary

ALPHABET LENGTH. The measurement in points of a complete lowercase alphabet in any type face and size. Used to determine the average characters per pica.

ASCENDER. That portion of a lowercase character that extends above the *X*-height.

AUTHOR'S ALTERATION (A/A). A change in textual matter which differs from the original material or instructions furnished to the printer, requested by the author or others and chargeable to the author or publisher.

AUTHOR'S PROOF. The master proof on which all errors, queries, editorial and factual corrections are accumulated.

BEN DAY. A shading medium used for the introduction of dots, lines, stipples, grains and other patterns into an illustration.

BLEED. The extension of printed images beyond the trim edge of a page layout.

BLOW-UP. The photographic enlargement of copy.

BODY COPY. The main body or text of a typographic page excluding the headline, subhead, signature and illustration captions.

BODY SIZE. In metal type, refers to the metal on which the type is cast, height and width.

BOLD FACE (BOLD) TYPE. A type face in which the weight of the strokes comprising each character is heavy (bold) when compared to the normal faces available in that same family of type.

BOOK DESIGN. The conception, planning, and specifying of the physical and visual attributes of a book.

C/C. Cap all important words.

CRT. Cathode Ray Tube often used for visual displaying of type being set.

CAPTION. Textual matter in the form of a word, phrase or sentence accompanying an illustration for the purpose of identification, description or clarification of the pictorial matter.

CARET. A small wedge (   ) used in correcting proofs to indicate the point of a correction to be made.

CASTOFF. The separation of galleys of type into individual pages.

CHARACTER. A single letter of the alphabet, numeric figure, punctuation mark or symbol.

CODEX. The first books in the form of bound leaves, as distinguished from the scrolls that preceded them.

COLD TYPE. A classification of typesetting processes originally applied only to direct impact methods (typewriter, varityper, etc.) but which now is broadened to include the various forms of photocomposition. The term *cold type* was coined to distinguish these processes from that known as *hot type*, a process of casting type from molten metal.

COMPOSITION. (1) The setting of type characters to form words, phrases and sentences for subsequent printing, (2) The transformation of original copy into a form suitable for printing or for making printing plates (metal type set by hand or machine, impact composition, photographic composition), (3) Cold type set in pages or in galleys with some effort toward both legibility and aesthetical considerations.

COMPOSITOR. A person who sets type.

CONDENSED TYPE. Type characters distinguished by a greater height-weight ratio (higher and spaced more closely together) than is exhibited by the regular or normal characters within the same type family.

COPY. The textual matter contained in any printed piece.

COPY FITTING. The determination of the amount of space to be occupied by manuscript copy after it is set in a specified type size, type face, leading and column width.

COPYHOLDER. The person who reads the copy aloud when proof reading.

COPY MEASURE. Instructions for typesetting which include the measure, type style, type size and leading. For example, 10 pt. Electra with a 2 pt. leading on a 25 pica line would be expressed as *Electra 10/12 x 25.*

CREDIT LINE. A statement accompanying an article, photograph, or drawing which sets forth the name of the author, artist, publisher, or copyright holder.

CROP. To remove, or indicate the removal of, those portions of a photograph or drawing which are not to be reproduced. The marks to indicate such information are called *crop marks* and are short lines made with grease pencil in the white edges surrounding a glossy photograph.

CURSIVE TYPE. A classification of type faces resembling handwriting.

DESCENDER. The part of a typographic letter extending below the base line formed by the middle segment of the letter occurring in the characters *g, j, p, q,* and *y.*

DISPLAY TYPE. Typography normally used for headlines and characterized by relatively large size in comparison with the size used for body copy.

DUMMY. A hand-sketched set of sheets of paper cut and bound or folded to indicate the size, shape, sequence, appearance, layout and contents of a publication to be printed.

EM. A unit used by typesetters and printers to measure the width of type letters, spaces, column sizes and page. An *em* is a square of the type size used, therefore it is a square. For example, a 12 point em is 12 points wide and 12 points deep. The symbol for an em is *M* or □.

EM SPACE (DASH). A space used for the separation of type matter, such as figures, equivalent to the width of an em of the type size used in setting the type.

END-OF-LINE DECISION. A decision required of the typesetter or compositor when justified type is being set and the end of a line of type is reached. Normally the interword spacing technique will allow the line to end with a complete word. Occasionally, however, this method results in a loose setting and leaves large and unsightly spaces between words. When this happens (or is apparent) the input operator will attempt to hyphenate the next word to fill out the line. If the next word is not subject to hyphenation, the operator must (1) rephrase the copy slightly, (2) reset preceding lines to a tighter or looser setting, or (3) accept the resultant poor spacing. Some systems circumvent this problem by varying interletter spacing.

EXTENDED (EXPANDED) TYPE. Type characters distinguished by a smaller height-weight ratio (wider than high) than is exhibited by the regular or normal characters of the same type.

FAMILY. A group of type faces bearing a resemblance to each other in design, character and aesthetic qualities, but varying in weight of the strokes, width of the body and general effect.

FLUSH INDENTION. A method of paragraphing in which each line of text in the paragraph measures the same width, with the possible exception of the last line.

FOLIO. A page number as it appears on the page of a book.

FONT. An assortment of alphabetic letters, numerals, characters and symbols which comprise a complete set of type in a specific point size and design.

FORMAT. The style and design of a book, or other publication, in regard to typography, paper, binding, layout, paper size, illustrative treatment and shape.

FULL MEASURE. A line(s) of type set to the full specified column width without any indention.

GALLEY (GALLEY PROOF). A single column of set type produced prior to paste-up or paging which is made available to the author or proofreader for correction.

GOTHIC TYPE. A classification of type characterized by the relative uniformity of weight in the stroking of the letters, and by the absence of serifs.

GUTTER. The inside margin, next to the binding edge of the page, of a book or other publication.

HAIRLINE. An extremely thin line or rule used in setting type such as a thin line to separate columns of type matter.

HALFTONE. A screened negative, velox or reproduction of a continuous tone photograph.

HEADLINE. A word, group of words or sentences usually set in relatively large display type above the body of the textual matter.

HOT TYPE. A typesetting process which involves casting type from molten metal.

IMPACT COMPOSITION. A form of *cold type* which involves impacting or striking characters directly from raised type keys onto paper. Examples include the typewriter, Varityper, and the IBM MTSC.

IMPOSITION. The arrangement of pages for printing on a single sheet of paper laid out in a pattern so that greatest economy may be obtained in respect to the number of press impressions required for the job.

INDENTION. A space left at the beginning of a line of printed matter as an indication of paragraphing.

INLINE TYPE. A style of typography distinguished by the appearance of a thin 'white' line within the contour or stroke of each character.

INPUT DEVICE. A keyboard mechanism similar to a typewriter on which characters are keyed and punched onto paper tape (or other media) for later feeding into a computer phototypesetter (called the output).

ITALIC TYPE. A style of typography distinguished by a slanting of each character toward the right.

JUSTIFY (JUSTIFICATION). The process of typesetting that results in vertically aligned right and left-hand margins rather than the uneven right-hand margins common with typewriter copy.

KERNING. The overlapping of certain type characters to avoid visually unattractive spacing.

LAYOUT. The drawing or sketch of a proposed printed piece.

LEADERS. Dashes or dots used to guide the eye across the page to an intended word or figure.

LEADING. The extra space allowed between lines of type. Pronounced *leding*, the space is normally expressed and measured in points.

LEGIBILITY. The quality of type (or writing) that makes it *possible* to read. (See *Readability*.)

LETTERSPACING. The spacing between each letter of a word.

LIGATURES. Combinations of characters in which two or more letters are joined into one.

LIGHTFACE TYPE. Typography in which the weight of the strokes comprising each character is light or thin when compared to the regular or normal face.

LINE COPY. Type, typewriter, pen-and-ink drawings, and other matter consisting of solid black and white areas (lines or dots) without shading.

LINE MEASURE. The width of a line of type expressed in picas.

LOGO (LOGOTYPE). Name of a product or company in a special design used as a trademark.

LOWER CASE. The small, uncapitalized letters of the alphabet (lc).

MAKEUP. The assembly of all elements of a page in their proper relationship.

MEASURE. The width or depth of type matter usually expressed in picas.

MEASUREMENTS. Within the type area are generally given in picas. Those outside (paper, illustrations and margins) are given in inches.

MECHANICAL. The final form of pages to be photographed, adhered to a white board or heavy paper, with all elements in correct position relative to each other and relative to the edge of the page. The preparation of a mechanical is the equivalent of *Makeup.*

MECHANICAL ART. The cutting, arranging and pasting of the various portions of a printed piece.

MODERN TYPE. A classification of typography which is distinguished from old-style Roman by greater regularity of shapes, more precise curves and delicate hairlines and serifs.

MONTAGE. A grouping of photographs each of which has been joined to the other, often without obvious demarcation.

NEGATIVE. A photographic, reverse image of original copy reproduced chemically on light sensitive film.

NUT DASH. A horizontal dash longer than a hyphen but shorter than an em dash.

OCR. Optical character recognition.

OPEN-FACE TYPE. A classification of typography distinguished by a partial outline effect for each character.

OPTICAL SPACING. Visual spacing (as opposed to actual mathematical point-unit spacing) between lines of type to achieve pleasing balance.

ORNAMENTS. Individual decorative or illustrative type elements.

OUTLINE TYPE. A classification of typography distinguished by the appearance of each character in outline form, rather than solid.

OVERHANGING INDENTION. A style of typesetting in which the first line of the textual matter has been set to the full measure and succeeding lines set to a smaller measure.

OVERLAY. A transparent or translucent sheet placed over copy on which work to be overprinted is prepared.

PE. Printer's error which will be corrected without charge by the printer.

PAGE PROOF. A copy of galley type arranged in final page form which is prepared for final proofing and correction prior to photographing.

PHOTOCOMPOSITION. Any form of composition utilizing a photographic image which is exposed by a light source onto sensitized photographic paper or film.

PICA. A unit of measurement of width and depth of lines of type equivalent to approximately 1/6 inch. Six picas are approximately equal to one inch (0.996″).

POINT. A unit of measurement of size of type faces, rules, borders, or other elements used in typography, equivalent to 0.013837″ or approximately 1/72 inch. 12 points equal one pica. 72 points are equal to 0.996″.

PROOFREAD. To examine the text appearing in a galley or page proof for the purpose of noting typographical errors, spacing errors, wrong fonts, etc., preparatory to printing.

PROOFREADER'S MARKS. Correction marks placed on a proof or copy to indicate errors or changes to be followed by the compositor.

PROOFS. Reproduction in some form of type or illustrations prepared for proofreading. May be *repros, whiteprints, blueprints, ozalids, vandykes, Brunings, Xeroxes, copywhites, etc.*

PROPORTIONAL SPACING. A term used to describe the spacing of type characters in which each character takes up an amount of space proportionate to its width. For example, a lowercase *i* may only require 2 units of space whereas an uppercase *H* may require 5 unites of space. In more highly sophisticated typesetting systems the unit variation may be considerably more refined. For example, in an 18 unit system a lowercase *i* may require 5 unites, a lowercase *x* 9 units, an uppercase *N* 13 units and an uppercase *W* 18 units.

QUAD. A combination of fixed spaces.

QUAD LEFT (RIGHT) (CENTER). A combination frequently encountered on the last line of a justified paragraph in which there are too few words to space out across the column. In this situation the words are quadded to the left (flush left) with a constant amount of interword spacing.

RAGGED SETTING. A typesetting method in which the spaces between words are uniform and the extra space needed to fill out a line is applied at the right (or left, or both right and left). Sometimes called *unjustified, flush right* or *flush left*. Typewriters, for example, normally produce a flush left ragged setting.

READABILITY. The characteristics of a body of type that makes it *comfortable* to read. Readability of a page is affected by: *typeface, type size, line length, leading, page pattern, margins, contrast between paper and type, typographic relationships, suitability to content.*

RECTO. A right-hand page.

REPRO (REPRO PROOF). A sheet of coated or very smooth paper on which type matter has been printed for purposes of photographing for printing.

RETOUCHING. The alteration or correction of a photograph.

RIVER. An irregular path or channel of white space in the midst of printed textual matter resulting from poor spacing and serving to interrupt the flow of reading.

ROMAN TYPE. A classification of typography partially derived from Roman inscriptions and letter designs, and usually categorized into two subdivisions: Old Style and Modern.

ROUGH. A preliminary, sketchily drawn layout designed to indicate the relative size and placement of the various units.

RULES. Elements of typography usually used as borders or separators in the form of straight or decorative lines.

RUN-AROUND. Type matter that does not measure the same width as previous lines, but which is narrower because it falls adjacent to an illustration, around which it runs.

RUN-IN CHAPTERS. Chapter openings that occur on the same page as the end of the preceding chapter.

RUNNING HEAD. Captions that run across the top of every page in a book or other publication.

SANS SERIF. A classification of typography characterized by the absence of small projections or serifs at the extremities of the letters. The term means "without serif."

SCALING. The process of determining the new size of an area which is to be photographically reduced or enlarged from its original size.

SCRIBING. Scraping off emulsion from an exposed and developed film negative with a pointed tool to form a line.

SERIF. The short cross-line or tick at the ends of the stroke of a Roman letter.

SET SOLID. To set lines of type close together, without leading.

SHADED TYPE. A classification of typography distinguished by the shading of the strokes comprising each character, rather than solid strokes.

SIDE BEARING. The non-printing area which is found to the left and right of the character itself.

SIGNATURE. A section of a book obtained by folding a single sheet into 8, 16, or more pages. (*See* Imposition.)

SINKAGE. The distance down from the topmost element on the type page, *not* from the edge of the page itself.

SMALL CAPS. An alphabet of small capital letters commonly used in combination with the larger capital letters. Frequently used in book composition for the initial words leading into a new chapter.

SPACE BREAKS. One or two line spaces in text.

SPACE OUT. To increase the spacing between words or lines to make a full length, or to cover a specified area.

STET. A proofreader's instruction to the typesetting indicating that a change previously made is to be disregarded and that the original is correct. The word is Latin for "let it stand."

STRAIGHT MATTER. Plain composition, in ordinary paragraph form, as distinguished from display or that set in a special arrangement.

STYLE. The optional points of grammatical usage.

SUBCAPTION. A word, phrase or sentence placed between two paragraphs of the main body of textual material for the purpose of breaking up unrelieved text, and to introduce a new thought which is expanded by the copy following the subcaption.

SYMMETRICAL DESIGN. Symmetrical arrangements are based on a common center axis with type centered on that axis. Asymmetrical arrangements also require balance but in a more optical, art-oriented sense and are not structured to a center axis.

SUPERIOR CHARACTER. A smaller type character placed adjacent to larger characters and used for reference purposes in mathematical terminology.

SWASH LETTERS. A capital letter of the alphabet characterized by flourishing and generous stroking, used at the beginning of a word or paragraph. It is designed to confer an elegant air to printed matter.

TEXT. The body matter of a book or other publication as distinguished from titles, headings, references, indexes and other auxiliary matter.

THIN SPACE. A space used to set two characters or symbols slightly apart by a constant amount.

TRADEBOOK. The conventional hardcover book sold to the general public.

TRANSPOSE. Type matter in the wrong position and noted in proofreading by *tr.*

TYPE FACE. A style or design of alphabetical letters, numerals, and other characters consisting of basic strokes that form the body of the character. Type faces are distinguished and identifiable by the weight of the strokes, the presence or absence of serifs, the angle and formation of the serifs, the ratio between the height and width of the letter, the degree of slant and other special designs.

TYPE PAGE. The area containing all of the printed elements on a page measured horizontally and vertically.

TYPE SIZE. Refers to the distance from top to bottom that includes the highest and lowest points in an alphabet.

TYPOGRAPHY. (1) The art of selecting, arranging and setting type, (2) the study of printing from type characters; the appearance or arrangement of printed matter.

U/C. Cap first letter and proper nouns only.

UNIFORM WIDTHS. A term used to describe the spacing of type characters in which each takes up the same amount of space, whether it is a punctuation mark, a capital *H*, or a lowercase *i*. Standard typewriters are designed to produce characters of uniform widths.

UPPERCASE. Capital letters of the alphabet.

VERSO. A left-hand page.

WIDOW. A short last line in a paragraph or a short line ending a paragraph at the top of a page in a book and generally consisting of one or two words.

WORD SPACE. To increase the distance between typeset words for the purpose of obtaining greater legibility and improving appearance.

X OR Z HEIGHT. The height above the base line of a lowercase character with no ascender.

INDEX